RA

FILLING THE VOID

Six

Steps

from Loss

to Fulfillment

DOROTHY BULLITT

Rawson Associates

RA

Rawson Associates

Scribner

Simon & Schuster Inc.

1230 Avenue of the Americas

New York, NY 10020

Copyright © 1996 by Dorothy Bullitt

Designed by Jenny Dossin

Set in Adobe Bodoni Book and Burlington

Manufactured in the United States of America

1   3   5   7   9   10   8   6   4   2

Library of Congress Cataloging-in-Publication Data is available.

ISBN 0-684-81869-8

To my mother, my hero

Author's Note

When my brother died I searched without success for a book that would give me perspective and hope. Over the years, following other losses, both personal and professional, I turned to a variety of books for guidance and comfort. Most helped, but none offered the comprehensive approach I sought. *Filling the Void* is the book I searched for but could not find.

Acknowledgments

Of the many who deserve my thanks, my mother, Kay Bullitt, deserves the most, for her inspiration, example, and advice. Also deserving of extraordinary appreciation is Nancy Antonelli, my friend and assistant, for her steadfast support and valuable suggestions and for patiently typing draft after draft of this manuscript.

Thanks to those who provided me with valuable editing advice early in the writing process: Jack McCullough, Barbara Wright, Jim Wickwire, Leigh Farrell, my sister, Margaret Bullitt, and my brother, Fred Nemo. For their support and suggestions along the way I thank Paula Selis, Bob Bowen, Dick Settle, Carol Molchior, Judith Pierce, Johanna Schorr, my aunt Margaret Baillie, and, in particular, my husband, Jim Hailey. I wish to thank my father, Stimson Bullitt, for his meticulous editing and for his excellent advice about the publishing process.

Thanks also to the many individuals who read early drafts of the manuscript and bolstered my confidence with their decision to share it with friends and relatives grieving a loss. In particular I want to thank those early readers who wrote me letters that helped me attract the publisher I most wanted and whose stories enrich the introduction. Special thanks to Tracy Steadman and Tim and Carol Kane.

The case studies that begin each chapter are true stories (in some, names have been changed) except for chapter 7, "Back-sliding," in which the case study is a composite. Many of the shorter anecdotes contained in the chapters are composites with fictitious names. Except for public figures, the individuals featured (and still living) have authorized me to include their stories. Thanks to all those individuals whose stories fill this book.

Finally, I want to thank my agent, Connie Clausen, and my publisher, Eleanor Rawson, for their advice, support, and conscientiousness. They made the publishing process a remarkably pleasant experience.

Contents

Filling the Void

Before You Begin This Book

The phone rang in the darkness. It was 4 A.M., the day before Thanksgiving. I bolted out of bed and grabbed the receiver. My father's gentle voice said, "I have some bad news. Ben drowned in the lake a few hours ago. His body hasn't been recovered yet. Mother and I went to the dock near where his friends say he went down, and we spoke with the police. They're searching for his body right now."

Ben was my brother. He was twenty-four. I was twenty-six.

Physically strong and strikingly handsome, with dark hair and blue eyes, Ben exuded animal magnetism. Raised in a family with a New England reserve, he always seemed more Mediterranean. Sometimes warm and charming, sometimes brash and antagonistic, Ben made an impact, both good and bad, on people. Impulsive and independent, adventurous and alluring to women, he blazed through his short life.

From his early teens, Ben used and sold marijuana. Eventually he turned to cocaine, a drug that quickly seduced him and came to dominate his life. During and after high school, he held a number of jobs. At twenty he opened and ran, with some success, his own antique furniture store. For fun he learned kung fu, climbed mountains, and courted women. A formidable downhill skier and a strong swimmer, he once swam nearly three miles from Seattle to Bellevue and back across Lake Washington, the lake in which he later drowned.

When he was twenty-two, a thirty-two-year-old wheeler-dealer (with a legal education and a pronounced southern accent) walked into his antiques store and changed his life. Ben, drawn to a glitzy high life foreign to our rather frugal, serious-minded family, found it with Willie, who swept him into a world of rented limousines, free spending, and cocaine. From the day I first met Willie, I sensed trouble and futilely tried to turn Ben away from him. My father tried, too, with equal futility. Though Ben was charismatic, intelligent, and charming, his worst qualities flourished in Willie's company. During his last few months, Ben and Willie began borrowing money from local banks, capitalizing on the bankers' perception of our family's wealth. They used the money to buy the boat from which Ben entered the lake and drowned on that November night.

The police did not recover Ben's body, so my father hired a private firm to search the lake. Days passed and it became apparent the search would fail. The lake was too deep, and although we tried again several times over the years, we never found him.

What actually happened on the boat that night remains a mystery. Within hours of his death, rumors began to circulate that Ben had not drowned by accident but rather had been murdered by Willie. The police investigated but never brought charges. Willie now resides in prison, serving time for unrelated crimes. He denies killing Ben; perhaps he didn't. He did, however, take out a murder contract on my father and me from the maximum-security unit of the county jail, convinced, it appears, we were behind his incarceration for robbery and aggravated first-degree murder. When the police learned about the contract they warned away the man Willie hired to kill us, and he left us alone.

Throughout the months following Ben's death, ugly reports filled the media. The large outstanding bank loans, combined with a missing body, caused many who never knew Ben to think he did not die, but rather sneaked away to some tropical paradise. For over ten years we listened to people say, "You don't really believe he's dead, do you?" We sometimes felt denied the chance to grieve.

Shortly after he drowned, my mother received a letter from someone who had been disappointed by a decision she once made while chairing a community project. Still bitter, the woman wrote that Mother deserved to lose her son and that, in her opinion, Ben's death was a good thing.

On the first anniversary of his drowning, she was shaken to find in her mailbox the ominous Tarot card of death.

Despite Ben's youthful tribulations, Mother always stood by him, loved him, and believed in his potential. The suddenness of his death, the sordid aftermath, and the absence of a body made losing him especially difficult. I watched her survive all of this with dignity and grace. She did this intuitively, without a conscious plan. During the worst times, sleeping, traveling, and listening to music helped her; so too did the comfort she received from our family and a few close friends. Every day she found time to spend in solitude, enjoying the simple pleasures of a lovely garden and a home with lots of natural light. In time she looked inward, and forgave those who had injured her. Then she reached out.

She joined the international peace movement: she helped produce a citizens' peace conference; traveled on Sister City missions to the Soviet Union, Nicaragua, and Africa; and founded an International Center. In the process, she formed many new relationships, traveled throughout the Third World, and received several distinguished peace and human rights awards.

More than anyone I know, my mother converts suffering and frustration into a force for good. She determines what she has to offer, moves outside herself, and gives what she can, without thought of personal gain or glory. When her marriage ended after twenty-five years, she found consolation in community service. Long committed to quality public education, she founded a partnership of private businesses and public schools which is still thriving fifteen years later. After her eldest granddaughter committed suicide, she helped found a coalition of citizens united against violence. And when relatives and friends stricken with terminal illnesses lay dying, she nursed them, helped organize their affairs, and comforted their loved ones.

Throughout my life, through all my ups and downs, my mother has been my greatest supporter, a reservoir of love, a source of strength, and a role model. For forty years I've watched her bounce back from self-doubt, frustration, disappointment, and despair. And now, as she enters her seventies, she's more full of life and purpose, more loved and loving, and happier than ever before. When I'm in troubled waters, I strive to follow her example and navigate my way to a calm shore.

My mother's approach to life's difficulties is intuitive. So, too, are those of many friends and colleagues, clients and acquaintances who have suffered severe losses but *successfully managed to fill the void inside themselves.* Most of these successes were achieved by ordinary people, faced with circumstances they did not choose or want, who filled their emptiness slowly, incrementally, with many stops and starts. In this book I try to break down these intuitive approaches into a set of steps all of us can use to travel from a state of emptiness and despair toward a state of fulfillment and joy.

■

The stories and suggestions that fill this book were drawn from personal experience. I recovered from the sudden deaths of my brother and niece, the untimely deaths of friends, the divorce of my parents, a traumatic job loss, and a broken engagement. I've counseled clients struggling with unemployment, retirement, and deep professional discontent. I've closely observed friends, family members, and acquaintances recover (or fail to recover) from the death of loved ones, divorce, abandonment, disability, grave illness, childhood abuse, poverty, and more. Our stories give this book its spirit.

Since the issues addressed by this book are universal, I've tried to make it accessible to men as well as women, young as well as old, and people of widely different backgrounds and circumstances.

The initial response of readers has both surprised and grati-fied me. During the past year, over a thousand people have read the manuscript. It has been passed around the country, with copies so far turning up in twenty-five states, as well as Canada, Australia, Germany, Italy, Israel, and England. As I had hoped, the book is helping people cope with different kinds of loss.

A middle-aged woman, whose husband had died of a heart attack as he slept beside her, read several books on grief but found all to be too long and laborious. She wanted something more accessible, so I offered her a copy of *Filling the Void.* She read it and emerged from her depression because the book gave her hope and a practical approach to survival and recovery. Her therapist was so surprised by the change in her outlook, he asked her what happened. She told him about the book and he asked for a copy. She gave copies to him and two of her friends. A stockbroker in the midst of a divorce, unable to find a book that could help him, asked if he could read mine. He read it straight through, high-lighted passages, immediately began implementing suggestions, and gave a copy to his estranged wife. A Russian immigrant, struggling with issues of identity, read the book in a single sitting and promptly gave copies to her husband and two of their friends.

When a couple's nineteen-year-old son committed suicide, a former neighbor gave them a copy of the manuscript. Two months after the young man's death, his stepfather wrote to me:

> Carol read your book the evening she received it and,
> at Carol's suggestion, I awoke early the next morn-
> ing to read it. Next to the unqualified love from fam-
> ily and friends, your book gave us guidance and hope
> at a time when both were wanting. We learned that

no matter how much we hurt at the moment, it
would abate and be assisted by reaching out rather
than in. Healing would take place best by our taking charge of the process, in minute steps at first but
taking charge nonetheless. This we have tried to do.

A therapist, estranged from her mother and conspicuously
absent from her stepfather's recent funeral, read the book shortly
after his death. An avid reader of books on healing and self-
improvement, she selected *Filling the Void* to send to her mother
in an effort to comfort her and pave the way for a reconciliation.
A professor in the midst of a midlife crisis read the book, immediately made some significant life changes, and gave a copy to
his twenty-two-year-old daughter. An executive, fired after
twelve years with her company, read the book and immediately
passed it along, first to her widowed mother and then to her husband (himself in a professional crisis). A minister's wife, generally uninterested in self-help books, read this one cover to cover,
and recited passages to her dying husband. Later, she gave
copies to grieving parishioners and several friends.

One reader wrote me the following letter about what the book
had done for her:

> I am a young mother in a new city with a new job.
> I've felt a void with my transition for almost a
> year. I am now starting to fill the void in my life.
>
> At times, life seemed an endless series of mun-
> dane tasks with nothing to look forward to but to run
> again for the next paycheck. *Filling the Void* gave me
> an organized way to find a path toward larger fulfill-
> ment. I read it in one sitting and felt that I could iden-
> tify with many of the examples. *Filling the Void* also
> reemphasized important points at the end of each
> chapter, making goals and action clear. I keep this
> book by my bedside and refer to it again and again.

I hope my book helps you.

1
Filling the Void

You may not know it, but at the far end of despair,
there is a white clearing where one is almost happy.
JEAN ANOUILH

- Do you feel a void inside yourself?

- Do you feel empty, depressed, or in despair?

- Are you grieving over a death or the end of a marriage?

- Were you fired from a job, or rejected by someone you love?

- Do you feel your identity disappearing in the midst of raising young children or in retirement?

- Are you seriously ill, recently disabled, or alone in a new place?

- Do you sense something important but elusive is missing from your work, your marriage, or your life?

All of you share something in common; some feel a deeper void than others, but the process of successfully filling it, however deep, is essentially the same for everyone. There are steps you can take, but they involve effort and patience. This process is not a quick fix; it is a way of life.

Six Steps to Fill the Void

There are six steps as you travel from emptiness to fulfillment. You will slide backward. The deeper the void you're trying to fill, the more often you'll slide backward. Since you must face up to your pain in order to fully recover, but can only endure it in bearable quantities, backsliding ensures you will continue to confront all the pain requiring your attention. So when you backslide, just start again—your cumulative progress will be greater than you think. Some steps will seem easier than others, and gradually the void will start to fill. In time, a sense of fulfillment will replace what you're feeling now. If you're willing to take these steps deliberately, even when they're difficult, the rewards will be great: you'll find the capacity to love deeply, feel keenly, act purposefully, and live fully. Do the work and *convert your emptiness into energy, your self-doubt into self-worth, your pain into power.*

In the following chapters I explore each of the six steps you need to take, illustrating them with stories of individuals who successfully filled the void inside themselves, and of others who gave up instead. Briefly, the steps are these:

Step One: Halting the Downward Spiral

Anyone whose heart is broken, identity lost, or reason for living forgotten will at times feel swept downward in an emotional spiral. When this happens, you need to halt the downward spiral, stabilize emotionally, and, for a while, stop consciously suffering. Different techniques work for different people, but all include nurturing the body, distracting the mind, soothing the soul, and reducing stress.

By halting the downward spiral, by stabilizing yourself emotionally, you enable yourself to move forward toward personal fulfillment and peace.

Step Two: Facing Your Pain

There is no magic pill. There is no Prince or Princess Charming who will come and solve all your problems. If you want to feel fulfilled, alive, and happy, you first must endure some pain. This may mean weeping, raging, and an aching heart. It may mean long stretches of feeling alone and unhappy. The alternative is to cut off your feelings, dull your senses, and shrink from life. In the end, if you avoid pain, you'll love less, feel less, be less. True fulfillment comes at some cost.

Some pain is so great it must be endured in small doses. Some voids are so deep they take a long time to fill. But, a willingness to gradually walk through the pain will bring you to a place where you are stronger and more alive, where you can look back over what happened without flinching, and without hiding from your memories.

Step Three: Looking Inward

By looking inward you can gain perspective, relieve yourself of bitterness, and start planning for a brighter future.

- Realize the door that slammed shut on you may not open again, so you need to start looking for an open window.

- Stop and look inside yourself for direction.

- Listen to your subconscious and try asking for guidance from a higher power.

- Let go of that which you most want to control.

- Forgive those who hurt you most deeply—don't endorse, condone, or excuse unconscionable behavior—but excise from your heart the resentment that holds you back and keeps you in darkness.

- *Forgive yourself.*

- Take an inventory. What are your skills, resources, desires? Are there aspects of yourself you don't fully express? What is missing from your life? What special, untapped talent do you have to offer?

Step Four: Looking Outward

Take that special talent and look outside yourself for ways to express it. This may be through community service or political activism, starting a business or painting a picture, changing jobs or starting a family. Are there people you could help who suffer in just the way you've suffered? Once you figure out what you can offer, look around for a complementary, unfilled niche: a community need, an untapped market, an audience for your creativity, a cause to promote.

Looking outward can help free you from gloomy self-absorption, moving you forward toward fulfillment.

Step Five: Sharing What You Have to Give

Once you've identified what you have to offer and who would appreciate it, start sharing. Help a neighbor, start a business, staff a hotline, join a choir. Opportunities will present themselves to you. Take them.

Step Six: Finding Fulfillment

If you endure pain in manageable doses, nurture your body, soothe your soul, identify what you have to offer, and conscientiously pursue a worthwhile purpose outside yourself, you can find fulfillment, feel alive, and make the world a better place in the process.

Key Points

- It is possible to move from the depths of emptiness and despair to fulfillment, even joy.

- The process involves patience, effort, and inevitable backsliding.

- "Filling the void" is a six-step process:

  1. *Halt the downward spiral.*

  2. *Face your pain.*

  3. *Look inward.*

  4. *Look outward.*

  5. *Share what you have to give.*

  6. *Find fulfillment.*

2

Halting the Downward Spiral

To keep a lamp burning we have to keep putting oil in it.
MOTHER TERESA

When Ruth lay on her hospital bed recovering from cancer surgery, her husband, Jon, came to her and said, "Would you find somewhere else to recuperate? I don't want you to come home." After eight years of marriage, he left her there in the hospital, and invited a younger, healthier woman to come live with him in what had been Ruth's home, Ruth's bed.

Jon sought perfection and was repelled by vulnerability. Had the surgery been unsuccessful, Ruth would have had to undergo chemotherapy with its accompanying nausea, hair loss, and exhaustion—and Jon was no caretaker. He expected his wife to support *him,* but lately she hadn't been as supportive as he liked.

The previous autumn Ruth had (at Jon's suggestion) entered a graduate program which, on top of her job, took most of her energy. As a result, she could no longer spend as much time entertaining Jon's colleagues or discussing his work as she had before.

Jon wanted a wife who was 100 percent with him. But a few months earlier, when he was in the midst of a bitter dispute with one of his children from a prior marriage, Ruth suggested he consider the child's point of view. Though she was just trying to help him reconcile with his daughter, Jon perceived what she did as an act of betrayal.

It was only in retrospect that Ruth realized that her illness, her absorption with school, and her efforts as family peacemaker had, in all probability, led Jon to another woman and the decision to leave. At the time, it all seemed shocking and unexpected.

Five months earlier, before she was sick, Ruth felt buoyed by the vitality of her marriage and her husband's love. Jon had surprised her with a Valentine's Day trip across the country, complete with roses and champagne. Theirs was not a decaying marriage. To Ruth, theirs was a marriage cut down in its prime.

Her orderly life ended in an instant. Still a successful executive, still loved by many friends, but with her health fragile, her heart broken, and her identity shattered, life to her seemed finished. The pain of betrayal and loss washed over Ruth, returning again and again. But when the pain got to be too much, she kept it from destroying her by halting the downward spiral.

Open, warm, and fiercely loyal, Ruth made friends quickly and for keeps. Childless, she had plenty of affection for the people around her and she gave love readily and generously. So it was no surprise, when Ruth was in despair, that her friends and colleagues were there to give her love and reason to hope. They reached out to her and Ruth accepted their support. Always the caretaker, now she allowed others to care for her. Friends provided her with a place to live and stood by ready to join her for dinner, a walk, or a trip to the movies. Employees, aware of their boss's heartbreaking loss, helped her out at work and kept the organization going when she couldn't concentrate.

A philosophical attitude about life and suffering derived from her college studies many years before, coupled with a natural self-discipline, helped her pull back from oblivion. Friends came up with various ways she could help herself feel better. In order to stabilize her emotions, she nurtured her body, soothed her soul, and distracted her mind. She visited a health spa, sought the support of a sensitive psychologist, spent time with those people who gave her energy, and avoided those who drained her. She read escapist literature and watched funny movies. Massage and facials became a regular part of her routine. Initially rendered passive by Jon's betrayal and abandonment, she became aware that big-muscle exercise can help ease depression, so she started swimming and running regularly with a friend from work. All of this helped her to regain her balance. Appreciative of the outpouring of love and kindness she received, Ruth felt she had a responsibility to survive.

After Jon first announced he was leaving her, Ruth tried to change his mind by suggesting marriage counseling and by offering to resume their relationship without questions or recrimination. But Jon was unreceptive to her overtures and filed for divorce.

By halting the downward spiral that had begun with her surgery, Ruth became sufficiently stable emotionally to endure the ugliness of divorce proceedings. In time she recovered from cancer, gradually healed her broken heart, and discovered a new identity. It took a commitment not to be bitter. She had seen the toll bitterness took on Jon's first wife, even though they had been divorced long before Ruth met him. Ruth knew that if she stayed bitter, happiness would forever elude her. For over a year she vented to her friends almost continuously. Gradually, as she began to focus on making a life better than the one she had lost, her anger began to subside. It helped that Jon was consistently unfriendly—had his old charm ever reappeared, it would have been harder. It helped that they reached a property settlement

Ruth felt was basically fair. And it helped that she hadn't lost everything—she still had a satisfying job and loyal friends.

Throughout her suffering, Ruth tried to live by the maxim that pain should be welcomed because it can teach us a lot. Afterward, she shared what she had learned with others who, like her, had been abandoned and betrayed.

A few years after Jon left her, Ruth realized she was happy and had been for a while. She married a man who had been introduced to her by her regular running and swimming companion, and they adopted a baby girl. Ruth's new husband is steadfast in his devotion, admiration, integrity, and love—and to his credit and hers, she trusts him.

•

In times of great suffering it may be tempting to escape through drugs, drinking, or gluttony, promiscuity or religious fanaticism, all routes destined to make things worse. Sometimes pain can become so severe it becomes difficult to eat, sleep, or function. In my experience, reducing external stress and maintaining good physical and spiritual health can control the downward spiral of despair.

Certain kinds of self-discipline can help. Even if you generally prefer an open-ended, spontaneous existence, you may find it helpful to build more structure into your life for a while. At times when I've felt most out of control, I've derived comfort from my daily routine. When I dreaded what the day had in store, routines as simple as a regular wake-up time, hot cereal, and a three-mile walk to work gave me reasons to rise in the morning. If you are living alone after years of companionship, your nights may feel long and lonely. Evening routines such as working out at an athletic club, joining a neighbor to walk your dogs, or visiting the local video store to return last night's film and select this evening's may transform a dark abyss into a structured, predictable, even comfortable stretch of time. A daily routine, like the sunrise and the seasons, may remind you, as it has me, of renewal and the pleasure of simply being alive.

At times of loss or disappointment, it is important to deliberately reduce the stress in your life. Avoid spending time with those who deplete your energy. Learn to say no. Make time to spend with people you enjoy and around whom you feel your best. Do away with nonessential obligations such as washing your car, corresponding with friends, or pruning your hedge, and take time out to "vegetate." Finally, counseling, as well as the spiritual guidance offered by church, synagogue, or private meditation, may provide valuable support in your effort to halt a downward emotional spiral.

If despair, fear, or emotional paralysis is overtaking you, you need to focus on regaining your balance. Begin by nurturing your body, distracting your mind, and soothing your soul.

Nurture Your Body

In the midst of a downward spiral, make a deliberate effort to eat moderate quantities of easy-to-digest and healthful food. Set plenty of time aside for rest and regular exercise: not necessarily high-pressure, goal-oriented exercise, but exercise designed to help you feel "alive," such as yoga, dance, or cross-country skiing.

In times of stress, it may be tempting to overeat. Though temporarily comforting, this strategy will probably make you feel worse, while a moderate, healthy diet can help you feel better.

Wendy loved her job and the people she worked with until changes at the top drastically altered the company's culture. Before long, her track record of honest, dedicated work as guardian of the company's accounts seemed forgotten. Challenged and criticized, her ability to manage the company's money routinely questioned by the young M.B.A.s now in charge, Wendy felt her health deteriorating. Then, just before her forty-eighth birthday, her doctor said if she cared about her health she should quit her job. So, with an aching heart and injured pride, she submitted her resignation. Simply too drained to immediately start working somewhere new, Wendy elected to take some time off to recuperate and consider her future. Having saved enough money to cover a year's expenses, she and her husband agreed that, after thirty years of work, she deserved a break.

In order to improve her health and stabilize emotionally, Wendy committed to drop fifty pounds before looking for another job. After radically changing her eating habits, Wendy tracked her progress with growing satisfaction. Losing weight became for her a measurement of her recovery from the humiliation she endured. Gradually she met her goal, and as she grew slimmer and more energetic, her spirits rose. Physically and psychologically rejuvenated, Wendy, who dreams of one day starting a business of her own, decided to work part-time and return to school.

■

During periods of great stress, you may find that sleep can be elusive or overabundant. If sleep eludes you, the following techniques may help:

- If traffic noise or too much silence keep you from sleeping, try wearing earplugs, turning on a fan, or playing white noise or ocean sounds at your bedside.

- If streetlamps or morning light rob you of sleep, a satin eye mask may solve the problem.

- Stop drinking coffee, caffeinated tea, or sodas after noon.

- Take a walk after dinner.

- Unplug the telephone and avoid doing stressful chores after 8:00 P.M.

- Cut out cheese, butter, red meat, and other hard-to-digest food from dinner.

- Approximately thirty minutes before you want to go to sleep, eat a small portion of a pure carbohydrate such as

cereal without milk, a granola bar, or a dry English
muffin.

- Reduce or eliminate alcohol consumption.

- Drink herbal teas designed to induce sleep.

- Take a hot bath before retiring.

- Listen to hypnotic tapes designed to relax you into sleep.

People react to stress differently. Depression sometimes
results not in sleeplessness but in overabundant, debilitating
sleep. If this is a problem for you, build additional structure into
your life in order to limit the hours you spend sleeping, and
increase your energy and level of activity. If you make yourself
attend an exercise class starting at 7:00 A.M., you'll sleep less
and do more. After work, if all you want to do is sleep, resist and
go for a walk or out to a movie instead. Like insomnia, excessive
sleepiness can be addressed by diet. By eating a limited quantity
of foods high in protein, moderate in carbohydrates, and low in
fat, you can increase both your mental and physical energy.

.

Good physical health can make you more emotionally resilient
and speed up the process of healing your soul. If you are open to
nontraditional medicine, visiting a naturopathic physician may
help you strengthen your immune system and improve your overall health. Other alternative treatments some will find useful
include: Reiki therapy, shiatsu massage, detoxifying treatments,
and foot reflexology.

Reiki and shiatsu focus on clearing the body of energy blocks.
The results of these treatments typically include increased
energy and the feeling of being more "centered" than before.
Seaweed and herbal baths and body wraps can pull toxins from
your body, increase your energy, and make you feel better.

Foot reflexology is an ancient science based upon the princi-
ple that reflexes in the feet correspond to every aspect of the

body. Sore spots in the feet indicate blocked energy in related parts of the body. When stimulated by thumbs and fingers, thousands of nerve endings in the feet conduct energy throughout the body, releasing blockages, relieving stress, and restoring balance.

To locate a naturopathic physician in your area, contact the American Association of Naturopathic Physicians, at 2366 Eastlake Avenue East, Seattle, Washington 98102. To locate a Reiki therapist, contact the Reiki Foundation, c/o Randall A. Hayward, Director, 2147 Oakland Drive, Kalamazoo, Michigan 49008. To locate a reflexologist, contact the International Institute of Foot Reflexology, at P.O. Box 12642, St. Petersburg, Florida 33733. Reflexology, shiatsu massage, and various detoxifying treatments are available at day and destination spas in many American and Canadian cities and in most resort towns. You may be able to learn more about the alternative therapies available in your area from staff at the local health food store, medical specialty store, or public library.

Neglecting your body in the midst of grief can cost you your health and delay your emotional recovery. After my brother died I stopped exercising, forgot to take vacations, and paid little attention to my diet or how much I slept. I got by fine for a while; then, eighteen months after his death, my health broke down and it took me years to recover my previous vitality. A decade later, reeling from another loss, I realized that while I could not stop my heart from aching, I might ease the pain by deliberately rejuvenating my body. In addition to making myself eat and sleep, at a time when I was inclined to do neither, I turned to Reiki, shiatsu, reflexology, and detoxifying baths to help restore the energy that grief had taken away. Body work picked up where reading and conventional therapy left off. When talking and thinking no longer helped me, body work did. These treatments helped me to feel "centered" and physically energetic, thereby improving my spirits and hastening my emotional recovery.

If you can't afford to pay for body work but want to try it nonetheless, borrow a book from the library on reflexology and practice on yourself, or ask a friend to work on you. (After my friend Bob had heart surgery, I gave him regular foot reflexology treatments, which helped him feel better and made me feel useful.) Trading regular back massages with a friend or relative may also help. And inexpensive mineral salts, available in any health food store, can provide you with detoxifying treatments in your own bathtub.

However you get there, a stronger, more energetic body and a positive body image will help you stabilize your emotions and halt the downward spiral.

Regular exercise can offer energy, exhilaration, and a release of tension. When Rachel walked out on Aaron six months after their wedding, Aaron felt crushed and humiliated. Caught in a downward spiral, Aaron quickly and deliberately stabilized himself. He converted his pain into physical power. He joined an athletic club and learned to play squash. When he wasn't working, he was practicing his sport, and in less than a year he was winning tournaments. With this physical evolution came renewed self-esteem, an emotional cleansing, and a fresh start. Aaron is now happily remarried and the father of two.

Strenuous exercise on the basketball or tennis court, the soccer field or running track, can help detoxify your body, calm you down, and cheer you up. You may also benefit from doing yoga or tai chi. Stretching and breathing exercises help many people feel more balanced and in control. If you are effectively housebound but still eager for exercise, why not try aerobics or yoga, guided by a video or television coach?

A positive body image can bolster your self-esteem. Facials, fresh haircuts or a new hair color, new clothes or a new pair of shoes may help halt the downward spiral. However, if you are worried about money, doing these things may nurture your body but ultimately depress you. Less expensive ways to feel good about your body when you feel worst about yourself include carefully grooming your face and hair, taking special healing or invigorating baths, and consciously choosing to wear your most becoming clothes.

Distract Your Mind

In the midst of a rapid downward spiral, survival may mean turning away from pain for a while. In order to stabilize emotionally, find nondestructive ways to distract your mind.

After Alan lost a bruising election, his spirits were crushed, his debts intimidating, and his future bleak. At first, he sat in the kitchen obsessing hysterically to his wife and wandered around the house slamming doors. Sometimes he stayed in bed all day, staring at the ceiling, too depressed to get up. Finally, his middle daughter convinced him to leave the house and distract himself.

He started going on movie marathons, three or four a week. This helped. He selected movies where he could escape into humor or adventure, and they distracted him for hours at a time. By temporarily distracting his busy mind from dwelling on his defeat, Alan started to get some perspective. He started exercising, helping around the house, gradually picking up the pieces of his career, and moving forward.

Escapist literature, board games, cards, baking, and redecorating all can help distract a tortured mind from suffering for a little while. Many people find playing with children a relief and a distraction. What distracts you? So long as you don't hurt yourself (e.g., with compulsive gambling) or anyone else in the process, seeking ways to distract your mind when your pain is unbearable will help you stabilize emotionally. Once stable you can return to face your pain again at a pace and in amounts you can bear.

Vent Your Anger Without Making Things Worse

Those who have been betrayed, humiliated, defeated, or abandoned face the challenge of managing inevitable anger without making things worse. Punching the nose of someone who injured you may feel good momentarily, but chances are you will compound your problems. Not so if you punch pillows, chop wood, or write letters never to be sent, as you fantasize revenge to your heart's content. Likewise, putting sugar in the gas tank of your ex-spouse's prize automobile may make you feel better—briefly—but it may also trigger retaliation or an unwelcome and expensive lawsuit.

Though you may feel like storming into a restaurant and screaming accusations at your former boss, doing so will probably get you in trouble. By contrast, screaming as you stand alone on a field or by the sea may help release your rage and free you to move on without the inevitable embarrassment of a public confrontation.

Relieve Yourself of Unnecessary Pressures

Coping with loss, disappointment, and anger takes energy. In order to maximize your available energy, try relieving yourself of unnecessary pressures.

Are there people in your life who drain you of energy? People you feel you must entertain? People who depress you with their vicious gossip or their incessant whining? People who always want something from you? Avoid these people. Make a point to spend your discretionary time with people who energize you, those with happy souls, optimistic outlooks, kind words for their neighbors, and big shoulders for you to lean on. This is a time to build up your reserves of energy.

Does the news depress you? The news on television, radio, magazines, and newspapers can pull down even the more cheerful among us. You may, therefore, want to take a vacation from the news during those times you feel especially low.

Is your work stressful? Individuals in high-pressure jobs can do much to halt a downward spiral by temporarily easing up at work. After my brother died, as an attorney I simply couldn't bring myself to enter a courtroom, cross-examine hostile witnesses, or argue with opposing counsel. My employer permitted me to spend a month outside of court, training a new lawyer and preparing her for the cases I was scheduled to try. This worked out well for both of us, and within a month I felt ready to return to battle.

If you are self-employed or fortunate enough to have a flexible and supportive boss, I encourage you to find ways to reduce the level of stress in your work for a while. It will be a good investment for all concerned.

Are there tasks around the house weighing you down? If you can, hire someone to take away these burdens. If you hate yardwork, hire a garden helper for a while. If your house is a mess and making you miserable, hire a part-time housekeeper. If you can't hire someone to relieve you of these and other pressures, consider a trade. Are there tasks you really enjoy doing? Do you know someone you could trade with? Could you bake bread in exchange for a mowed lawn? Paint a fence in exchange for a clean house? Give a back massage in exchange for an hour of ironing? Be creative. Relieving yourself of unnecessary pressures can help you halt the downward spiral.

Soothe Your Soul

Though different approaches work for different people, accepting support from those who care, finding purpose through small, simple accomplishments, and gaining perspective and inspiration from nature usually help to soothe the soul.

Those of us who are self-reliant and unused to receiving care can benefit from learning to accept support. I used to be more comfortable caring for others than receiving care, but I learned to rely on my friends during hard times. When the man I hoped to marry broke my heart, two older women friends reached out and comforted me. I was twenty-three, inexperienced, and convinced I would never recover. Without condescension, they assured me I would. They told me of their own romantic disappointments, took me out for meals, and gave me the book *Surviving the Loss of a Love* to guide and console me. They treated my heartbreak as serious and deserving of sympathy while simultaneously demonstrating their conviction that I would soon be fine. And they were right.

Later, when my brother died, the letters, calls, and visits of condolence I received from friends and acquaintances, particularly those who themselves had lost relatives, were extremely helpful. One woman wrote of losing her brother though he was still alive. Manic-depressive and addicted to drugs, he had spent the prior year in a mental institution. Her brother was my brother's age; we'd all known each other in earlier, happier times. By sharing with me her sadness, she lessened mine. A former professor of mine sent me a little card with the simple message "in deepest sympathy," the stark simplicity of which moved and comforted me. My closest friend, whose brother had committed suicide six years before, came to me as soon as she heard the news that Ben was dead. She said, "Now we have both lost our brothers." She made me feel part of a club—a club composed of all those people who'd lost someone they loved—and I no longer felt alone.

When Adam, a high-profile executive recently fired by his employer of fifteen years, sat alone in his makeshift office, staring into space, it was a call from a fellow Rotarian that rescued him from hopelessness and despair. She came to Adam's office and escorted him to a Rotary Club meeting. As they walked through the downtown streets past shops and office towers, she told him about her despair after being fired a decade before, and about how she picked up the pieces. (She landed a job running a small, struggling company which she built into a large and profitable business.) Exuding confidence in Adam's abilities and professional options, she enthusiastically offered her assistance in his search. Her openness and generosity warmed and encouraged Adam, who never felt quite as desolate again.

When Lemar, recently separated from his wife and desperately missing his kids, received an invitation from a basketball pal to play poker with a group of friends, he gratefully accepted, contrary to his natural inclination to remain private. Though he had friendly acquaintances at work and the gym, Lemar told no one about his separation. One of the ball players learned from his wife (who'd heard from a friend of Lemar's ex) that Lemar was now living alone. Insisting that he must be lonely, she persuaded her husband to invite Lemar to join the poker game held at their home every Friday night.

Lonesome, but uncomfortable initiating social contact of any kind, Lemar appreciated being drawn out of his seclusion. He started playing poker every week, coming as much for the company of the host's wife and kids as for the game itself. He wrestled with the boys, sang to the little girl, and hung out in the kitchen, talking to his hosts about how much he missed his children. They enjoyed Lemar's company, felt good about helping him out, and, as he adjusted to his situation, a mutual friendship gradually evolved.

■

Soothing the soul often involves a Zen-like pursuit of small accomplishments such as organizing a cupboard, cleaning paint brushes, packing a box for the Salvation Army, or repairing a vacuum cleaner. By doing this you may block out your burdens for a while. Cooking, shopping for groceries, cleaning the kitchen, or making a bed are the kinds of tasks that if voluntarily accomplished, without frustration, help center a tormented soul.

Meditation, music, and natural beauty may help you endure hard times. Some people, calmed by the familiar liturgy and music and a sense of community, find comfort attending church, mosque, or synagogue. Others prefer private meditation. Listening to music deepens despair for some, but for others it lifts up their hearts and fills their souls. For some, gardening is a burden, to others a source of serenity and renewal. Time spent around trees, lakes, and wildlife may be emotionally healing and restorative; so, too, may be a visit to the desert, the mountains, or the sea.

■

Pets are, for many, a great solace. A dog, a cat, a bird, a fish—whatever your preference, it may help. During the thirty years

Ellen and her husband Sol spent raising a family and building a business their lives grew tightly intertwined. When Sol died, he left a dog who became for Ellen a beloved companion, a reminder of the man she missed, an antidote to loneliness.

When Tracy's father left, the apartment seemed empty. As the only child of working parents, she had often felt lonely, but this was worse. Eager to comfort their daughter as they went about ending their marriage, her parents gave Tracy a cat. He slept on her bed, joined her in the kitchen for meals, and curled up beside her when she did her homework. She loved her cat and, as her parents had hoped, he helped her endure the worst aspects of their divorce.

> *What soap is for the body humor is for the soul.*
> YIDDISH PROVERB

Humor can help you. Norman Cousins, former editor of *The Saturday Review,* used humor to cure himself of a crippling illness. He watched funny movies and episodes of *Candid Camera.* He surrounded himself with comedy and laughed his way back to good health. "I have seen what laughter can do," Bob Hope observed. "It can transform almost unbearable tears into something bearable, even hopeful." So search for ways to find humor in your heartache. If you can't, search for humor in the world around you and soothe your troubled soul.

How we soothe our souls is particularly personal. Think back—what worked for you before? Telling jokes? Playing golf? Singing songs? Reading poems? If it worked for you before, try it now—emphatically!

Help Others in the Same Boat

Misery loves company. People suffering from the same loss or disappointment can help each other endure the hardest times.

When Carlos's and Tony's parents fought, separated, and then struggled over custody, the brothers found comfort in consoling one another. They shared their fears, their sorrow, and their anger. When one felt he deserved blame for his parents' divorce, the other assured him he was not to blame. Each boy understood how the other felt, and together they felt calmer and more philosophical.

When a family of four was murdered at home by a stranger, the families living nearby were traumatized. Shaken, frightened, and confused, the neighbors pulled together. They held community meetings, ran errands, performed mindless but necessary tasks, and tried to help the police in any way they could. By keeping busy and helping each other, the neighbors managed their grief and succeeded in keeping their fears from spiraling out of control.

Coworkers suffering under a tyrannical boss kept their self-esteem from disappearing altogether by supporting one another. When the boss targeted Aisha for abuse and humiliation, her coworkers reminded her she was not the problem. They said, "Remember what happened to us last week." They assured her she was worthwhile and competent. And the next time, when their boss targeted someone new, Aisha made a point to reach out to that person.

Seek Help from an Expert

Nurturing your body, distracting your mind, relieving yourself of unnecessary pressures, and soothing your soul should help you stabilize emotionally. If you lack a support system or simply feel too exhausted to take the initiative to employ any of these techniques, consider seeking out the support of a psychologist, psychotherapist, or self-help group. If you're grieving a death, a grief counselor or grief workshop may help. If you're agonizing over a divorce, consider joining a divorce support group. If you were sexually abused, an incest survivor's group may offer what you need. For nearly every loss there is a support group. If groups are not your style, call an experienced therapist for individualized assistance.

Once you halt the downward spiral, you can start traveling from pain toward liberation and peace.

Key Points

- In order to halt the downward spiral, turn away from your pain for a while in order to stabilize your emotions.

- Useful techniques include:

Nurturing your body

Distracting your mind

Venting your anger in ways that don't make things worse

Relieving yourself of unnecessary pressures

Soothing your soul

Helping others in the same boat

Seeking help from trained professionals

3

Using Your Pain
to Start The Healing

We are healed of suffering only by experiencing it to the full.
MARCEL PROUST

Instead of meeting her dad for lunch as planned, Crystal bought a bus ticket to Los Angeles. She disembarked in Eugene, Oregon, and checked into a motel room where she doused herself with gasoline and lit a match. Two men in the hall outside heard the explosion, broke down the door, and put out the fire. When Crystal arrived at the hospital where she was born twenty-two years before, burns covered 100 percent of her body.

The previous summer, a friend of Crystal's was killed by neo-Nazis. On the afternoon of his murder, when she saw her friend in the unlikely company of the skinheads, he had signaled to her for help. But she misinterpreted his gesture as grandstanding and flirtatious, and went home. Later, she felt deeply responsible for what happened, believing that but for her vanity and cowardice she might have saved him. Anguished, she told her father that she, like Japanese author Yukio Mishima (who ultimately committed *sepukku* to avoid disgrace), was searching for honor.

Upon hearing what had happened the night before, my mother, sister, niece, and I rushed to Portland. When we entered the waiting room outside the burn unit, I observed an old man, shriveled and gray, weeping pitifully as he stood alone in the center of the room. What a sad old man, I thought. The old man was my forty-three-year-old brother, Fred, transformed by agony. We stayed with Crystal during the last hours of her life. She lingered a night and a day with no sign of consciousness. Fred likened her suicide to the self-immolation of Buddhist monks during the Vietnam War. In both cases the motive was sacrifice and the acts were intended to send messages. He was convinced that Crystal had wanted to do something as courageous as the murder of her friend had been cowardly. He believed she wanted to help turn the tide against hate crimes.

My brother is a visual artist but for most of his adult life his main identity has been that of full-time single parent. When his eldest daughter, an avant-garde poet and dancer, committed suicide, he was devastated. I've never seen such grief.

Fred did not grieve in quiet isolation. He threw himself into his work as the featured dancer/performance artist in a popular punk rock band. And in the months following Crystal's death, he frequently felt her presence when he performed. Fred found himself using his loss as a source of artistic power. Dance became a vehicle for coping with his grief, a way to channel it into something positive and creative.

He faced his pain. (According to Fred, he had no other choice.) He wept and raged—the elements of anger and sorrow in his performances were made to order for expressing his grief. He did not numb himself to suffering or flee from it. In addition to dealing with his despair through dance, he spent many sessions in a bereavement support group with other parents of children who had died violently that same autumn.

The University of Washington nursing school, which is studying the varieties of grief support for parents of children who have suffered sudden or violent deaths, located Fred through Crystal's obituary and invited him to attend their ten-week course. The program provided him with an invaluable constellation of information and advice, and the opportunity to reciprocate support with other bereaved parents. Working with counselors, they moved together through stages of their grief.

In addition to the bereavement workshop, Fred drew strength from his partner, Sara, a constant source of love, support, and sympathy. And, at a time when he felt no one had ever sustained a greater loss, one of his friends helped give him perspective. He told Fred a story about a woman he knew whose teenaged daughter had committed suicide right in front of her. In an instant, Fred realized he was not unique in the harshness of his suffering, but rather one of many bereaved parents devastated by the loss of a child.

Fred confronted his pain humbly and head-on. He deliberately filled the void left by Crystal's suicide with positive, life-affirming activities, determined to draw spirituality and strength from her sacrifice. In addition to dance, art, and political activism, Fred stayed involved in the lives of his surviving daughters and granddaughters.

Since Crystal's death, I've observed a dramatic change in Fred. He still grieves, but now when he enters a room, he fills it with his vitality, confidence, and personal power. Out of the ashes, he emerged a more substantial man.

■

Everybody experiences pain, loss, and disappointment. Some are crushed under its weight. Some numb themselves to avoid suffering. But some convert their pain into power.

Feeling pain is the step we all want to avoid following a loss or disappointment. We want our anger, hopelessness, and despair to disappear. We search for a magic pill to take away our resentment, self-blame, and feelings of uselessness. And when we see only darkness at the end of the tunnel, no exit to the maze in which we feel trapped, we just want to feel better, as quickly as possible. But in order to reach the sun, we first must walk through the rain.

Enduring Pain Is Not Easy

The choice to endure rather than avoid pain is not easy. At the time, avoidance may seem the more attractive option. But in the long run, avoidance makes things worse; facing up to the challenge makes things better.

Fred and my mother each faced the pain of losing a child and, in time, found they could endure what at first seemed unendurable. By avoiding the temptation to flee from their suffering they turned loss into a catalyst for creativity and community service.

Those who face up to their pain can look back with confidence that they made the right choice. But making that choice is by no means easy, so many choose to numb themselves instead.

Numbing Oneself to Pain Can Be Expensive

As Luther's wife, Jonquette, succumbed to breast cancer, he started drinking heavily. He could not imagine life without her. She was his home, his conscience, his reason for living. After her death, Luther's drinking increased, numbing the pain but in the process driving away family and friends and ultimately costing him his job. In an effort to avoid pain, he compounded his loss.

Inez survived her son's fatal illness by shutting off her suffering, but she, too, paid a price. A mother of three teenage children, Inez tried to keep the household going as normally as possible during her oldest son's brief, hideous illness, and after his death. When she wasn't at work, she busied herself with cooking and cleaning, and did her best to keep up the family's spirits. In the midst of tending to her dying son, surviving children, husband, and employer, Inez had no time to spare for her own grief. So she blocked it out. But numbing herself to painful memories had the unintended side effect of blocking out memories of her son's upbringing, of the years when her family was all together, still healthy, happy, and full of hope.

For a year and a half Andrea tried to please her boyfriend. Though she is big-boned and buxom, her beau preferred women who were willowy and model-slim. So Andrea dieted furiously, striving for a body to please him. Despite her efforts, he continued eyeing svelte models and rollerskating nymphettes with an undisguised admiration he never gave her. Andrea felt needy and unappealing. When he said he simply didn't find her attractive, they broke up.

Heartsick and humiliated, she numbed herself by bingeing on sweets, quickly ballooning into a very fat woman. Food gave her fleeting comfort, but instead of dealing with her loss, bolstering her self-confidence, and striking out on a course likely to lead her to a new companion, she took a route destined to lead her in the opposite direction. Far from getting better, Andrea's life was getting worse.

A close friend asked Andrea if she would join her at Overeaters Anonymous. Andrea agreed and began the slow process of healing. She began by confronting the pain of losing her boyfriend. Then she examined the patterns in her life which caused her to escape from pain in pints of ice cream, and which led her to a relationship with someone who would never really appreciate her. This process proved difficult but cathartic, and, in time, Andrea's compulsion to overeat subsided.

She began the process of building a better, more self-confident life. This involved changing her daily routine to include a four-mile run every evening after she returned from work—the time of day when, nervous and weary, she used to wander around her apartment and graze. Running simultaneously calmed and exhilarated her, and, instead of increasing her appetite, actually reduced it. As her body grew slimmer and stronger, her energy increased and her focus started shifting from her deficiencies to her potential. Every time she started feeling like a victim she stopped herself and concentrated on the power she possessed to make her life better.

Increasingly restless in her job marketing a product she no longer found interesting, Andrea decided to stop complaining and quit as soon as she could find a more challenging job. Eager to pass on what she had learned in the process of tackling her own addiction to food, Andrea found rewarding work counseling men and women with eating disorders.

Pain Can Result from Feeling Trapped in a Difficult Situation

Refusal to confront painful consequences can compound a loss and increase suffering. Facing up to it, though difficult, will ultimately bring freedom from pain and a new beginning.

Pain often results from feeling trapped in a difficult situation. A middle manager disillusioned by the changing rules and harsh new culture of his company, or a wife who hates her life after years of conforming to her husband's unyielding expectations, faces the choice of remaining where they are or leaving to make different, potentially better lives somewhere else. Leaving may result in financial distress and a temporary loss of identity. But facing disappointment, redefining success, and finding new ways to be useful and worthwhile may bring each a level of fulfillment their current course denies.

Andrew, an Atlanta executive, is a big, strapping, handsome man. For many years he enjoyed his work and liked himself. But when his company merged with another, larger corporation, this changed. Almost overnight the company became harsh and cold, and an atmosphere of fear, calculation, and contempt replaced the former atmosphere of trust and mutual respect.

A father with young children and a mortgage, Andrew felt he could not leave. In order to get along, he started compromising his values. Previously open with his employees, he became secretive and fiercely possessive of the few fragments of company policy top management allowed him to know. Once warm toward his colleagues, he grew cold, harsh, and increasingly self-centered. He couldn't understand why those who used to respect him now viewed him skeptically, with barely concealed disappointment and growing dislike. Gradually, Andrew realized he had no support left among his peers, superiors, or staff. All alone, he felt confused and depressed, still holding on to an image of himself no longer real to anyone but him.

Andrew's heart gradually hardened and his once striking personal presence began to fade. When he rose in the morning, he felt no joy, no hope, no genuine pride.

Unable to make the deliberate choice to leave, Andrew eventually left involuntarily, in a company reorganization. At first embarrassed and scared, he started over. He took advantage of outplacement counseling offered by his employer and spent a month exploring his interests, strengths, and undeveloped talents. Long interested in classic films, Andrew decided to use his generous severance payment to purchase a specialty video business. Despite a slow start, with much financial anxiety and some concern about his diminished status, Andrew succeeded in his new business. Having been trained as an accountant, he felt comfortable with the administrative and financial aspects of the enterprise. He hired staff with experience in the video business and a flair for selecting and promoting films. His obvious enthusiasm for old films helped him connect with his employees and attract a loyal clientele. As his own boss, his best qualities gradually revived. Once more happy in his work, Andrew faced up to the compromises he had made when he was miserable and afraid. He apologized to many of those he had hurt, forgave himself, and, once again, became a man he could be proud of, a father his children could admire.

■

Married with two children, Deanna couldn't remember when she last felt content. Dutifully she kept the house, chauffeured the kids to their appointments, and worked part-time to make ends meet. She no longer found her husband, Isaac, appealing and sometimes wondered if she ever had. As a teenager, Deanna had done well in school, never used drugs, or caused her parents any serious concern. Unlike her sister, "the disappointment," she was a "good girl." (No one in her family, except, of course, her sister, had been divorced.)

Still eager for her family's approval, Deanna put on a happy face and glossed over the frustrations of her marriage. Her parents, unaware of his uglier traits, liked Isaac. Deanna knew he slept around, put her down to his friends at work, and yelled at her in front of the kids. But the prospect of leaving him terrified her. So, she dulled her feelings, lost her sex drive, and spent a lot of time criticizing other people's life-styles and personal choices, while taking no action to try to improve her own marriage. Friends no longer called or visited. At work, she became known as a critical busybody, and lost one ally after another.

Deanna began to realize that by maintaining a facade of a marriage long dead, she'd become lonely and self-loathing, hopeless and frightened. And when she most yearned for sympathy, she received none.

Her boss, a compassionate, tactful man, suggested Deanna seek counseling and recommended a psychologist he himself had seen. At first she was defensive, since his recommendation related to the problems she was having with her coworkers. But she knew her boss's suggestion was made out of kindness, not contempt, and things certainly weren't getting better on their own. So, she decided to give therapy a try. In the beginning, she tried playing the victim but her therapist would not let her. He repeatedly confronted Deanna's assumptions about her parents, her marriage, her work relationships, and herself. The timing was right—Deanna was ready to change her own behavior if doing so might bring her a happier life. So she began rethinking how she approached her relationships. With difficulty, she assumed more personal responsibility for how her life was going and began disentangling her self-image from her parents' expectations.

She faced up to the fact that having stayed and done nothing to improve her marriage, she shared responsibility for its demise. Realizing it was too far gone to be revived, Deanna decided she must leave the marriage if she were ever to regain the qualities that once made her proud to be herself and happy to be alive. After determining that her children, damaged by the current situation, would fare better relating to their parents separately, she made a deliberate choice to leave the marriage. Consciously prepared to face her family's inevitable criticism, accepting the risks leaving entailed, she discovered divorce actually hurt less than the years of deadening herself to her marriage and to life.

.

Work and marriage are not the only situations in which an individual can feel trapped. When Sam was a child his father abused him. Angry and isolated, he seriously considered joining a gang. Instead he joined Boy's Club, where he found people who supported him and constructive activities that engaged his interest. One volunteer in particular took an interest in Sam. Andy spent hours talking with him about the problems he was having at home. He told Sam about his own adolescence—how he, too, had been beaten and berated by an abusive father. Andy gave Sam hope when he explained how most of his pain disappeared once he left home and found it in his heart to forgive his father.

Realizing that his dad was just repeating a pattern passed down from generation to generation, Andy decided if he were ever to become a better parent than his father, he must first break the pattern of abuse. To do this, he needed to forgive his father and consciously learn how to be a good parent. Making the decision to change was just the beginning of a long, difficult process—he still had to confront his pain. Bitter tears and rage were

followed by months of prayer and introspection, but in time
Andy forgave his father.

By deliberately spending time around well-adjusted adults
who knew how to nurture children, Andy learned what it meant
to be a good parent. Only then did he marry and have children of
his own. When Sam asked him why he volunteered at Boy's Club
Andy explained that he did so in the hope he could help a boy
like Sam find the happiness and satisfaction he had found.

Andy persuaded Sam to coach the preteen softball team and
help teach an art class. He proved to be a natural leader to whom
the children were devoted, and their easy, unambiguous affection fostered in him a new and unfamiliar tenderness. Although
at the time he pretended not to care, these Boy's Club experiences greatly bolstered Sam's self-esteem. Years passed before
he had enough distance from his family to follow in Andy's foot-
steps. But when he faced up to his childhood pain and forgave
his father, Sam, like his mentor, became a happier and more
peaceful person, eager to reach out to the next generation.

∎

If you remain in a workplace or a relationship that is strikingly at
odds with your conscience, aspirations, or sense of self, you may
find the compromises involved in staying result in a hardened
heart and a fading soul. Those who passively remain in an intol-
erable situation may, in time, seem to shrink, their power dimin-
ish, and their prospect of ever feeling real joy again dwindle.
Making a hard choice and facing pain directly may be the only
way you will find the happiness you seek.

If you are in a difficult situation, choosing to leave means
accepting pain in the short run in expectation of long-term gain,
while staying and doing nothing means accepting a slow erosion
of your soul and a darkening future. If you believe there remains
hope in your current situation you may reasonably decide to stay
and try to improve it, though making this choice means accepting risk. If you are willing to endure immediate discomfort for a
happier life in the long run, you are well positioned *to stay and*

strive to make your situation better. Whether you stay or leave, deciding to strive for a better life involves *the willingness to experience loss and endure some pain.* If you stay and do nothing, you will bear pain of a different kind—a perpetual low-grade pain flowing from impotence.

There is no costless choice, no choice without consequences. Evaluate the risks each of your options entails and then consciously select one.

Those Willing to Face Their Pain Will Reap Rewards

Proust wrote, "We are healed of suffering only by experiencing it to the full." Those who confront their suffering directly generally emerge stronger and more alive than before. It seems unfair for bad things to happen to those who live virtuous lives and play by the rules, but life isn't fair and bad things happen to everyone. *Experiencing loss and disappointment is not about fairness, it's about being human.* Each of us faces the challenge of converting the burden weighing us down into a force propelling us forward.

History is full of examples of people who, by enduring pain, became great. Franklin Roosevelt, a privileged *bon vivant* in his youth, learned to empathize with the suffering of those in need after polio crippled him. Though he endured great physical pain, he reached out to the downtrodden and raised America out of the Great Depression. Harriet Tubman, beaten to the brink of death, recovered sufficiently (despite frequent blackouts) to escape from slavery and bravely lead other slaves along the underground railroad to freedom. Presidential Press Secretary Jim Brady, brain-damaged by a bullet intended for President Reagan, did not give up and wallow in self-pity. Instead he committed his life in a wheelchair to pushing for gun control legislation.

Insight, empathy, and a sense of purpose, clearer priorities and the feeling that "nothing can hurt me now," are among the rewards that flow from a willingness to endure. Once healed, we can look back without hiding from our memories and without fear.

Loss, betrayal, disappointment, and defeat all hurt and leave behind a void. In order to fill that void we must be willing to feel some pain, sometimes a lot of pain, as we gradually exchange the bitterness that lines it with something sweet and plentiful. This may happen slowly; the deeper the void, the longer it can take. But there is light at the end of the tunnel. There is a way out of the maze.

Key Points:

- You will be healed of suffering only by experiencing it to the full.

- There is no magic pill.

- The costs of avoiding pain by denying it can include dulled feelings, loss of memory, a hardened heart, and a fading soul.

- Bad things happen to everyone. Living a virtuous life and playing by the rules can not insulate you from loss and disappointment.

- The challenge is to convert the burden weighing you down into a force propelling you forward.

- Those who confront their suffering directly, who walk through their pain, will generally emerge stronger and more alive than before.

- There is light at the end of the tunnel.

4

Looking Inward

When we are unable to find tranquility within ourselves,
it is useless to seek it elsewhere.
LA ROCHEFOUCAULD

For years Merle dreamed of falling.

Merle loved machines. Coordinated and strong, he handled them with ease. He looked for work that would allow him to spend time around machinery, the more challenging the better. When Merle got his first job, as a rope-tow operator at a ski area just south of the Canadian border, the ski industry was young but technologically promising. Only seventeen years old and still in high school, Merle found the machinery easy to manage.

He advanced quickly in the ski business, his ability as a machinist earning him ever more challenging work. In his spare time, he flew planes and skied. Nearly every aspect of his life required a strong back, arms, and legs, and he viewed himself as a man whose work would always be physical.

At twenty-seven, while welding a chairlift, Merle fell forty-two

feet and broke his back. He could no longer ski. He could no
longer pilot a plane. And never again did he dream of falling.
His doctors told him he would never walk again. For six months
he couldn't, and then he defied them. Though he feels nothing
below his knees, Merle exerted his enormous will and taught
himself to walk with braces and a cane.

He looked inward for an answer to the question "If I can't be
the man I was, doing what I did, who can I be? What can I do?"
After inventorying his talents and determining which aspects of
himself were undeveloped or unexpressed, he decided that if he
couldn't make his living with his body, he'd make it using his
mind. Over the next several years, he taught himself to write and
speak effectively, and discovered he possessed natural talents
for business, leadership, and public speaking. He entered a
management track at the ski area, gradually learning all there
was to know about the business, and eventually became the general manager of a multistate ski-area corporation.

I worked with Merle for seven years, and though technically I
was his boss, he taught me much of what I know about business.
He also taught me it is possible to lose one's identity in an
instant, and rebuild a life full of dignity, achievement, and pride.

Looking Inward Is Hard Work

Once you stabilize yourself emotionally, start looking inward. In
order to fully recover from your loss or disappointment, to fill the
empty void inside, you first must do some challenging internal
work.

This process may involve letting go of that which you most want
to control. It may require forgiving yourself and others for seemingly unforgivable actions, listening to your subconscious, and seeking guidance and support from a higher power. As you proceed,
nature may prove a source of inspiration and perspective; art and
books may give you guidance and facilitate your introspection.

Finally, before you move along to the next step, you may profit, as Merle did, from inventorying your talents and determining which aspects of yourself are unexpressed and how you might express them.

Let Go of That which You Most Want to Control

When one door of happiness closes, another opens,
but often we look so long at the closed door that we
do not see the one that has been opened for us.
HELEN KELLER

If you've recently lost a job, a marriage, or a loved one, your health, your youth, or your dream, you may spend a lot of time dwelling on what might have been, looking back at the door that closed, trying to figure out how to open it again. Letting go is hard. But repeatedly reliving irreversible events leading up to your child's death or your husband's car wreck, your lover's departure or your sudden job loss, is harder. *You cannot undo the past, but you can affect the future.*

When Juanita lost her job of many years, her friends urged her to try something new. Reeling from her disappointment, she insisted the only job she wanted was the one she'd lost. She futilely tried to replicate what she had. Her insistence on looking backward and her inability or unwillingness to consider a different kind of work was a formula for more defeat and disappointment. Too many non-negotiable requirements regarding salary, status, location, mix of responsibilities, and type of employer prevented this talented woman from doing any useful work for a long time and plunged her deeper into despair.

By contrast, Patrick—fired at the same time—willingly undertook part-time work and a consulting project. He used his skills while retaining time and energy to explore other, more desirable options. This helped him heal and move on.

If you've lost a job once central to your self-image, you may suddenly feel desolate, stripped of identity and self-worth. But the period between jobs need not be all bad. It can be a time to define an identity independent of employment, income, and the approval of others. It can be a time for identifying basic values and goals, and redefining success in order to better employ those values and achieve those goals. This process need not be simply intellectual but can be spiritual and physical as well. It can be a time for meditation and reflection, a time for regular exercise and a healthier diet, a time to start living a life more consistent with your beliefs. This may involve finding a job that pays less but allows you time for civic causes, family, or more creative pursuits. It may mean redefining compensation to mean more than simply money. Perhaps you'll start a business of your own. But first, you must let go of the unchangeable past.

■

When Dan fell in love with a woman at work he still tried to preserve his marriage and be a good dad. For two years he juggled these two significant, full-time relationships. Then his wife found out and, in understandable distress, insisted he make a choice. At first he left her for his lover. But the havoc this caused, the uproar and criticism from his relatives and coworkers, drove him back to his marriage.

Then his lover found someone new and Dan fell apart. Grief-stricken, tormented by what he'd lost, he regretted deeply his decision to return home. Duty tasted bitter; he couldn't remember any good reasons why he returned home. All he could think about was that the woman he loved now slept in the arms of another man. In the midst of this crisis, Dan told his wife of his despair over losing the other woman, and again their marriage started to unravel.

Thanks to a forceful therapist and his own survival instinct, Dan began focusing on his real options: staying in his marriage, trying to heal its wounds—or leaving to live alone without expectation of winning his lover back. He realized if he kept obsessing about the woman he had lost, he would probably lose his family as well. So he started focusing on whether or not to stay in the marriage.

Throughout this difficult period, Dan's wife gave him support and understanding. He decided to keep his family intact and work to make his marriage happier. And though he continued quietly grieving his loss, he no longer threatened his future with futile regrets over what he could not change.

Letting Go of the Unchangeable Past Will Let You Move Forward

Letting go of the past will let you move forward. Various techniques may help you gradually let go. Some of my most controlling friends found ways of letting go by reading Eastern— particularly Buddhist and Taoist—philosophy.

For some, dreams will help guide the way. Diligently writing down or dictating dreams when you first wake up will help you remember them. Dream workshops, books on dream interpretation, or conversations with others interested in dreams can help you discern their meaning. In their book *The Dreamers Dictionary: The Complete Guide to Interpreting Your Dreams,*[*] Lady Stearn Robinson and Tom Corbett wrote,

> To interpret dreams you must bear in mind that the first step is to learn to distinguish between a valid prophetic dream and one that has no subconscious or clairvoyant significance. Dreams of a prophetic nature usually occur to you during the deepest part of your night's sleep; for most of you this will be between 2:00 A.M. and 7:00 A.M. By this time digestion has usually been completed, your body muscles are normally relaxed, and your mind is

*Published in May 1974 by Taplinger Publishing Co. and Warner Books by arrangement with Taplinger Publishing Co.

mainly free of the day's events. Dreams which occur under these conditions are generally worth your efforts at interpretation . . . The interpretation of dreams, like any other skill, becomes more interesting with practice. Perseverance is essential in learning a new language, and dream symbols are a language of the subconscious mind . . .

In order to interpret your dreams with some degree of accuracy, you must remember that dreams are made up of many elements. There is usually one main factor or feature that will stand out in your memory and that is the one which you should consider first; but you should look at all the other elements as well and add them to the interpretation . . . According to Aristotle, *the skillful interpreter of dreams is he who has the faculty of observing resemblances.* Try to cultivate that faculty and you will soon become adept at understanding what your dreams mean.

As you become more adept at dream interpretation, try asking your subconscious to let go of what holds you back. Dr. Stanley Krippner of the Maimonides Medical Center Dream Laboratory suggests that we can use our dreams to expose problems we refuse to recognize consciously and, by doing so, move toward positive, corrective action. As you drift off to sleep, ask your subconscious to figure out what you should do next, what path you should take. In the morning, you may discover you feel less burdened by the past, more flexible about your options, and more confident about the future.

Asking for support from a higher power can help you let go of what you most want to control. Once when I was deeply distraught and, like Dan and Juanita, kept trying to open a door closed to me forever, my sister Margaret gave me some advice. She said, "Before you go to sleep at night, ask for guidance and support." Skeptical but desperate, I did what she suggested. And it worked. Night after night I asked for help, and gradually I was able to let go of the disturbing memories that were obsessing me and move forward.

Forgive Those Upon Whom You Waste Precious Energy, Fruitlessly Resenting

Asking for help from a higher power can also help you forgive when forgiveness seems impossible. When you feel depressed and angry and without hope because of a great injury or, like Dan, great self-disgust and deep regret, forgiveness is necessary for you to move forward. Forgiveness does not mean forgetting what happened. It does not mean condoning or endorsing what may be an abhorrent act by someone against you or by you against another. When I speak of forgiveness I mean the process of excising from your heart the bitterness, resentment, or regret holding you back.

Nelson Mandela unjustly spent twenty-seven years in jail, but when he became president of South Africa, he invited his jailer to stand beside him as he took the oath of office. Think of the glow Mandela radiates. That is a glow I've seen shining from others, people who successfully forgave those who trespassed against them and learned from the injuries they sustained.

For years Helen could not function sexually, eat normally, or feel happiness; when she was thirteen, her father had molested her. Consumed with guilt and anger, Helen could hardly function. With the help of a skilled therapist, Helen decided that if she were ever to find happiness she must let go of the feelings caused by her father's great betrayal. She confronted him with what he did and how he hurt her. He acknowledged his actions and the pain she felt, but *didn't really apologize*. Still, the acknowledgment helped.

Helen read books about forgiveness. She prayed to forgive her

father and to rid herself of guilt. But for a long time her anger
was too great. Encouraged by her therapist, Helen wrote out her
options: estrangement from her father (and, consequently, most
of her family) or conscious reconciliation. Estrangement was no
longer acceptable—she wanted to return to her family, to attend
weddings and funerals without feeling nauseous, to share old,
familiar traditions, and, once again, have roots.

But before she could reconcile with her father, she knew she
must somehow excise from their relationship her obsession with
his earlier betrayal. Helen had to compartmentalize and destroy
the forty-year-old man, smelling of liquor, who had abused her
thirty years before. At her therapist's suggestion, Helen and a
friend went to a shooting range where she identified a cardboard
figure as her father—not the old man she knew now, but the
hard-drinking younger man who had violated her so long ago.
She shot it again and again, eventually obliterating the picture
and releasing her anger.

But Helen needed to do more than vent her anger if she were
ever to establish a comfortable relationship with her father—she
needed to focus on what she liked about him. In a clothbound
journal she listed memories of the best times: childhood visits to
his office, camping trips, the dog shows they attended every
summer. Helen realized that, unlike most of the other incest survivors she knew from group therapy, she had many positive
memories about her father. He was often warm, witty, and, in
spite of what happened, generally quite dependable. If he were
to die suddenly, she knew that, haunted by her good memories,
she would grieve bitterly about their estrangement.

Glad she had confronted her father about the worst part of
their relationship, she decided it would be healing to acknowl-
edge the best as well. So she sent him a letter describing her
happiest childhood memories. He was deeply grateful and, less
defensive than when she had confronted him, at last said he was
sorry. Though Helen appreciated his apology, it no longer mattered to her as much as she had anticipated. Instead, it was the

power she felt from having forgiven him that caused the black
cloud which had been over her so long to start lifting away.

Forgive Yourself

Sometimes, in order to forgive others for their trespasses against
you, you must first accept your share of responsibility for a problem and then forgive yourself.

A "blameless wife" left by her husband may find it hard to move
on without first facing up to the part she played in the demise of
her marriage. Was she always the giver, the caretaker, the accom-
modator? If so, she may have helped to create a relationship in
which she maintained moral superiority, leaving her husband in
the unenviable position of always feeling morally inferior. A marriage can fail for many reasons, but rarely is one party entirely
blameless. Differences about money, children, religion, or sex
may doom a marriage, but the spouse who finally leaves may not
be the only one responsible for its breaking up. If you played some
part in creating an irreconcilable relationship, face up to it and then
forgive yourself. Doing so will make it easier to forgive others, help
you resolve conflicts, and allow you to move on.

An adult child still furious with his dead mother over various
betrayals and disappointments may find it difficult to accept her
death if he, in fact, contributed to their troubled relationship. If this
is the case, accepting his share of responsibility for their problems
and acknowledging what their relationship actually was and what
it never will be will help him move beyond his anger. Because as
the saying goes, *"Forgiveness is giving up all hope for a better past."*

Life Is Not Orderly and Predictable

After a great loss, betrayal, or disappointment, letting go of what
might or should have been can be a slow, arduous, and counter-

intuitive process. Life *should* be fair. Life *should* be orderly. But alas it is not. I was reminded of this fact recently when a close friend suffered a heart attack and underwent quintuple bypass surgery. Bob is a trim, youthful forty-eight years old. He doesn't smoke, rarely drinks, consumes a healthy diet, and lives a relatively low-stress existence. He *should not* have had a heart attack. But he did.

Life is not the orderly, controllable garden we like to think it is. Life more closely resembles a forest or a flood plain. Trees die and make room for new growth. Natural fires erupt, destroying acres of beautiful wilderness, leaving ash in which new life will flourish. Like a flood plain, life can exist for a long time, seemingly calm and unchanging, when suddenly uncontrollable floods come, instantly transforming it into something entirely different. But like the forest after a fire, a flood will cover the plain with fertile soil fostering new life.

As difficult as upheaval is to an individual used to an orderly and predictable life, fallow periods can be equally stressful to an individual used to action and achievement. The bleak period following a divorce, job loss, death, or defeat may, to the high achiever, seem evidence of failure and a sign that life will always be difficult. Be patient. It will get better. Remember, for crops to flourish the ground must sometimes lay fallow.

Art and Nature Can Offer Insight and Perspective

Spending time in and around nature may offer perspective as you look inward. Walking in a garden, notice how the death of one season's plants makes way for the next wave of bloom. Build a sand castle on an ocean beach and watch the tide take it away. The fact that a life ends prematurely or a couple divorces or a career is cut short does not make the life, the marriage, or the career valueless. Like a sand castle whose beauty is undiminished by its short existence, relationships, experiences, chapters in life are not made worthless by ending earlier than desired.

Art may give you insight. Following a death or the loss of a love relationship, literature, films, plays, and poetry may prove a great help to you. Many artists use their particular medium to express and examine the experience of loss, disappointment, and renewal. What touches you? Poetry? Plays? Films? Music? If one medium particularly resonates with you, seek it out during this time of introspection. Love poems written by brokenhearted lovers throughout the centuries may give you comfort and perspective. Literature of mourning written by those who lost a child, a spouse, a parent, a friend may help you deal with your grief and make you feel less alone, part of a larger human experience.

When Brian lost his job in a corporate shakeup, his first thoughts were to sue, fight, right the injustice, and somehow get back his job. His wife reminded him that, legally, his employers could terminate him at will. Just or not, suing, she argued, would be futile. But Brian loved his job, his staff, and the company, in spite of his differences with the new folks in power. He couldn't stop wanting to turn back the clock.

A month after Brian was fired, he went to a film, *Mississippi Masala,* which traced the story of an Indian lawyer and his family driven from their native Uganda. The lawyer left a thriving career, friends, a beautiful home, and the country he loved when a political directive swept away the only life he'd ever known. He and his family settled in the United States, but he could not focus on the present or the future. Instead, he dwelled on the past, the injustices of his losses and his quest to regain his property. But his quest was futile. And by dwelling so long on what he could never change, he effectively lost twenty years of his life. In the end he realized he couldn't go back or right the wrongs. Sometimes justice simply isn't attainable.

After the movie, Brian returned home and wept for what he'd lost, at last accepting there was no point in fighting a battle he

could not win. With sadness, he turned away from the unchangeable past and focused on the future within his power to affect.

Therapy and Relevant Self-Help Books

As you look inward, books may help. Are you angry or
depressed? If you feel depressed you may be pushing rage
inward. Have you a constructive channel for your anger? If not,
find a way to let it go. Books on anger and depression may help
you sort through your feelings and move on. If you feel bitter or
resentful, look through a bookstore or library self-help section
for books on forgiveness. Even if forgiveness seems out of the
question, read a few pages and decide whether you can make
yourself read a book or two on the topic. If you can, do it. It will
probably help.

In addition to books on a variety of subjects, a psychologist,
psychotherapist, or self-help group may also help chart your
course of recovery. As you look inward you need not be alone.
Spiritual, literary, and professional guides can assist you on your
journey of self-examination and improvement.

Keep a Journal

Consider keeping a journal. It can be a friend to confide in when
you have no one to talk to. It can be a place to pour out your grief
and vent your anger, to boast of your accomplishments and
dream of a better future. It need not be elaborate, gracefully written, or bound like a book. Something as simple as a collection of
thoughts scribbled on scraps of paper, stuffed in a file, can help
give you perspective, sort out your feelings, set goals, and make
plans. Though you may never go back and read what you wrote,
the act of writing can help you focus your thoughts and plan for
the future.

Take an Inventory of Your Talents

What are your talents, skills, resources, and desires? What aspects of yourself are undeveloped or unexpressed? Does your life seem out of balance, devoid of spirituality, professional gratification, or artistic expression? Do you feel self-centered, without close friends, without outlets for tenderness or generosity?

Whatever your situation, spend some time contemplating (and writing down) what you're good at, what you enjoy doing, and what you long to do. What special talents, skills, or resources do you possess? Are you using them at work, at home, or in the community? If not, could you?

Do you feel bored and discontented at work? Does your work permit you to use and develop your special talents? When you work do you feel you make a contribution? If the answer to these questions is no, perhaps a career change is warranted. Consider visiting a career counselor—perhaps another career would better tap your talents and give you a greater sense of purpose and usefulness. If a job change is unrealistic, what about some volunteer work once or twice a month using those undeveloped or unexpressed skills?

Carol felt out of balance. Being a lawyer wasn't enough. A partner in her firm and by all measures successful, Carol still wanted something more. Increasingly drawn to the countryside, she decided to find a way to supplement her work as a lawyer with some physical outdoor work. She scaled back to a four-day week and worked the fifth day as a rural postal carrier delivering mail to farms on quiet country roads.

Ian looked inward and concluded most of his problems stemmed from his excessive self-absorption. Though successful in his career and financially well off, he felt there must be something more. He wanted to fill the emptiness inside himself; he needed a sense of purpose and a greater connection with other people. So he started giving money to charity and volunteered at a hospice for people with AIDS.

Figure Out What's Missing

What's missing and where might you find it? Your heart should
reveal what's missing from your life; your mind should lead you
to solutions. As a child, did you enjoy drawing, painting, wood-
working, or pottery? What became of those artistic impulses?
Does the prospect of attending a ceramics or drawing class at the
community center appeal to you? If so, sign up. Do you feel
smothered by your work? Do you yearn for action and risk? Have
you considered mountain climbing or joining a volunteer fire-
fighting brigade? What about coaching a basketball team for
inner-city kids? Do you feel depressed about aging, down on
your body, and running out of steam? Do you exercise regularly?
If not, set aside time for regular exercise. Are you cooped up all
week in the city? Find time to spend around natural beauty.

Do you feel solely responsible for your circumstances, fate,
and future? If this bothers you, why not try asking for guidance
quietly as you drift off to sleep? Are you lonely? Do you feel
unloving and unloved? Without expectations, try extending
yourself to an elderly neighbor or a coworker in need. Consider
volunteering at a soup kitchen for the homeless or reading to the
blind. Reaching out to others may help you feel more connected.
But also think about whether you've ignored any significant
losses or disappointments. If so, your feelings of lovelessness
may flow from your decision to numb yourself to pain. Are you
ready to face up to that old pain in order to regain your capacity
to give and receive love?

If You Can't Be Who You Were, Who Can You Be?

If you can't be who you were, doing what you did, what can you
do? Who can you be? The questions Merle asked himself after

his disabling fall are questions you should ask yourself if your marriage is over, your job a memory, your health impaired, your youth departed. Carefully consider these questions as you chart a course to a new and brighter future.

When a door shuts on you, another one will open before long. Stay observant. *It will appear.* As you wander around in a maze seemingly without an exit, remember: there *is* an exit. *Keep looking.* In the darkness of loss and despair, you may feel you will never see the light again, but you will. Stay alert, opportunities will present themselves. Seize them. Focus on your strengths and on what you can do to improve your own life. Stay open to change; it may not be exactly what you *want*, but it may bring you *what you need.*

Key Points:

- Looking inward is hard work.

- Life is neither fair, orderly, nor predictable.

- Music, art, creative activities, nature, self-help books, and therapy can offer insight, perspective, and assistance.

- Let go of what you cannot control.

- Forgive those whom you resent; don't waste precious energy.

- When one door shuts on you, another will open before long.

- As you wander around in a maze, seemingly without an exit, remember there *is* an exit.

- Keep a journal.

- Inventory your talents, interests, and resources.

Determine what aspects of yourself are undeveloped or unexpressed and figure out ways to express them. Doing this in writing will help you generate ideas and sort out your feelings.

- Stay open to change. It may not be what you want, but it may bring you what you need.

5
Looking Outward

The man is only half himself, the other half is his expression.
RALPH WALDO EMERSON

Discontented with her marriage and tired of her job as a massage therapist, Christine felt grumpy and restless. She knew something important but elusive was missing from her life. Looking around for answers, she learned about a workshop that might help. She spent two weekends with a group of men and women who, like her, searched for direction and a greater sense of purpose. The workshop caused Christine to shift her perspective: she stopped dwelling on her problems and started focusing on what she had to offer.

Remembering the joy she once derived from drawing, painting, and graphic design, Christine realized she needed ways to express herself artistically in order to feel happier and more complete. She looked outward for artistic opportunities. When she mentioned her objective to a friend, he told her about a portrait painting class. She signed up and quickly demonstrated considerable talent. Reading newspaper want-ads, she found another way to share her artistic gifts: the local transit system wanted artists to paint murals on its bus shelters. Christine prepared her portfolio and a written application, presented them to a review board, and received the chance to paint a mural.

That mural led to others. First she worked for free; later, people paid her to paint. In addition to enhancing bus shelters, her murals now brighten a community center and the walls of a store. She shares a studio with some other painters. Sometimes Christine teams up on projects with other artists. Sometimes she works alone, continuing to develop as a portrait painter. Her reputation as an artist keeps growing, and her life, once so out of balance and unsatisfactory, feels more harmonious and complete.

Newly energized, Christine feels better about her work as a massage therapist now that she can offer more of herself to her clients. The marriage is over but life overall is better because she determined what was missing, looked outside herself for opportunities, and found ways to express and share her gifts.

·

The unhappiest people I know are the most self-absorbed; the happiest are those who reach out and make a positive difference in the world around them.

Find Opportunities to Share What You Have to Offer

Once you've looked inward, freed yourself of some emotional baggage, turned away from the past and toward the future, and identified what talents lie dormant within you waiting to be expressed, you are ready to look outward. The purpose of looking outward is to find opportunities to share what you have to offer. Like Christine, this may mean searching for ways to express yourself artistically. It may mean seeking out neighbors or friends in need whom you can help. You may find opportunities to share your talents in a church or on a political campaign. If you relate more easily to animals than people, you may elect to adopt a dog in need of love and care. Maybe you'll look for a business opportunity. Or, like my mother, you may search out opportunities to serve your community.

Role Models May Help

If you feel uncertain about how to begin, start with role models. Who are your role models? Have they given to charity? Served their community? Expressed themselves artistically? If you admired your father and he volunteered for the March of Dimes, perhaps you could, too. If your favorite sports figure coaches Little League baseball, maybe you could coach a team as well. If you felt inspired when a coworker published some short stories, why not try writing something yourself?

Focus on an External Need, an Unfilled Niche

Focus on an external need, an unfilled niche. Is there a place for you to make a difference? If you want to perform community service, look through your phone book—it should contain a list of local community service agencies. If something looks interesting, call and find out if you can volunteer.

Films, newspapers, news radio, even TV sitcoms may give you ideas. Be alert to signs and directions from these and other sources. Mention your interest to friends and coworkers. They may suggest ways for you to share what you have to offer. Once you decide you want to reach out, opportunities will present themselves. Stay alert. Stay flexible.

Personal Hardship May Lead You to Ways to Contribute

Personal hardship may lead you to opportunities. If your daughter was suddenly abandoned by her husband and left without resources, it may help *you* to prepare meals and run errands for her and her children. If you want to do more, you could contact the local YWCA and see if there are things you could do for other women in similar circumstances, such as helping them prepare to reenter the workforce. If you grieve over your inability to bear children, consider volunteering as a Big Sister or a Big Brother to a child in need. If you recently survived a bout with cancer, consider volunteering to share your experiences with patients recently diagnosed with the same disease.

Personal hardship led fifteen-year-old Paul to help his community. When his family migrated to this country, he was eleven. Busy learning English, seeking work, and simply surviving in a new culture, Paul's parents forgot about their son. So Paul joined a gang. And members of the gang became family and gave support to him and to each other. But they also hurt people. Increasingly ensnared in a life of crime, Paul decided there must be a better way. He and other immigrant teenagers in the same position created a club designed to teach immigrant parents how to better support their children and keep them out of gangs.

A desire to honor the memory of someone you loved may inspire you. Sylvia and Sara lived together for nearly twenty years, during which Sara played cello in the local symphony orchestra. When Sara died of bone cancer, Sylvia missed her terribly. A year after Sara's death, the president of the symphony asked Sylvia to join the board. A desire to honor her partner's memory by supporting what had been her life work inspired Sylvia to throw herself into fund-raising, event planning, and other promotional activities on behalf of the orchestra. Doing this, Sylvia felt useful, appreciated, and close to Sara.

Unemployment or discontent at work may lead you to make valuable contributions. Ida felt increasingly discontented with her work and longed for more purpose in her life. She looked outward for ways to be useful. By volunteering evenings and weekends as a Girl Scout leader (as her mother had), Ida grew happier and felt much more balanced.

Climbing the walls after two months of unemployment, Peter felt desperate to use his skills and to feel a sense of purpose and accomplishment. A friend just starting up a retail business couldn't pay him but said she'd nonetheless appreciate his help. So Peter volunteered twenty hours a week, setting up his friend's accounting system and researching merchandise. When the business began to flourish, Peter's appreciative friend hired him full-time.

Loneliness may lead you to someone in need of care and companionship. Loneliness led Esther to become a surrogate grandmother to some children in her neighborhood. After their own children were raised and away at college, Esther's husband left her for a younger woman. Though she worked part-time, her job gave her no real sense of purpose—as raising children had. She longed for the days when she welcomed her kids home from school with cocoa and cinnamon toast. For Esther, bliss was playing Monopoly with a pair of nine-year-olds or sewing clothes for someone's favorite doll.

So when Esther noticed that several children living in her apartment building appeared to be on their own after school, she asked their parents if she might invite the kids to "tea." Delighted, they encouraged their children to accept Esther's invitation. Their first visit led to many more—a couple of the smaller kids came by nearly every day. Esther served homemade treats and read stories. Some days they played games, other days they worked on craft or cooking projects, occasionally they did homework. Before long Esther began feeling useful again, appreciated, and less lonely.

Helping others who hurt as you have may hasten your own

recovery. Kate owned and ran a nail station in a beauty salon where she gave manicures. At home, her husband beat her. When she got pregnant, she concluded he would only get worse. Unwilling to raise a child in so destructive an environment, she decided to leave. With the help of a friend, she escaped to a battered women's shelter. They counseled and comforted her and gave her a plane ticket to get to her mother's. She left behind her nail station and nearly all her possessions. Mourning the loss of her relationship, she started looking outward. Supporting her child, providing him with a healthy, stable environment, became her goal. As part of a battered-women's support group, Kate gained the confidence to start over. Gradually she healed her broken heart and rebuilt her self-esteem. She helped other women recovering from domestic abuse and resumed her career as a manicurist.

> *Let your hook always be cast;*
> *In the pool where you*
> *Least expect it, there*
> *Will be a fish.*
> O V I D

Once you determine what you have to offer, look outward for opportunities to share them. Focus on an external need, an unfilled niche. As you search for ways to contribute, stay alert to opportunities. Think about what your role models have done; you may choose to emulate them. Look for signs and direction in films, newspapers, radio, and TV. Mention what you're trying to do to your friends and coworkers. They may give you valuable leads. If you have the time, investigate multiple options. And consider the ways in which you've suffered. Are there things you could do to alleviate the pain of others who suffer as you have? As you help others by extending yourself, you will help yourself in the process. Free yourself from self-absorption, reach out, and find fulfillment.

Key Points:

- Films, newspapers, and TV may help you find opportunities to share what you have to offer.

- A desire to honor the memory of someone you loved may inspire you.

- Role models, friends, and coworkers may suggest opportunities.

- Focus on an external need, an unfilled niche.

- Personal hardship may lead you to opportunities for fulfillment.

6

Sharing What We Have to Give

If I can stop one heart from breaking,
I shall not live in vain;
If I can ease one life the aching,
Or cool one pain,
Or help one fainting robin
Into his nest again,
I shall not live in vain.

EMILY DICKINSON

G ary was my first friend to die of AIDS. During his long illness, his partner, Michael, himself HIV positive, nursed
Gary with loving tenderness. When Gary died, Michael
responded by dedicating himself to the service of others. Though
he continued working as an actor, he cut back and became a
therapist and Reiki practitioner, counseling and comforting
clients through touch. People with AIDS and their survivors
were also helped by a film he codirected about gracefully living

with and dying of AIDS. A few years after Gary died, Michael met and fell in love with Kevin, with whom he lived for several happy years before finally developing full-blown AIDS. At first he fought the disease, then he found peace.

As Michael lay dying, I realized solace would, for me, come from serving him. So I asked him specifically what he wanted to eat that was unavailable in the hospital. "Popsicles," he said. So I sent over a dozen within an hour. When I asked what caused him the greatest anxiety as he approached death, he said, "Covering the cost of my medical insurance deductible." So I paid the deductible. I asked him what I could do to help him feel free to let go and die peacefully. Worried about Kevin, who had developed a brain tumor, Michael said he wished there was a graceful way to invite his friends to cover the costs of the memorial service, cremation, and a few months of mortgage payments in order to relieve Kevin of that pressure. I offered to set up, advertise, and administer a memorial fund in Michael's name to cover these expenses. This delighted him. I set up the fund and nearly a hundred friends and relatives made donations. Not only were all the costs Michael mentioned covered, but also the uninsured aspects of Kevin's successful brain surgery six months later.

Michael wanted Kevin recognized as his partner in the newspaper; he wanted Gary remembered, too. I submitted Michael's obituary to several papers along with letters urging them to write an article about this remarkable man. They did—and both of his partners were recognized.

Throughout this, I felt useful. By telling me how I could help, Michael gave me a gift. He comforted all of us who loved him, and helped us accept his death. His memorial service was packed with friends and family, and Michael, the actor, received a standing ovation.

■

Once you've turned away from the past and toward the future, identified what talents dwell within you, and identified opportunities to express them, you, like Michael, will be ready to share what you have to give.

An Unwillingness to Share Makes Happiness Unlikely

Some people are unable or unwilling to share what they have to offer. And as they hoard what they have, they long for what they're missing. We all know individuals who feel empty and unhappy but take no constructive steps to make themselves feel better. They truly believe other people bear responsibility for their happiness and for filling the void they feel inside. But this is work we each must undertake alone. If we wait for others to make us happy, we may wait forever.

Mary is elegant, healthy, and financially secure. But the void inside her seems almost bottomless. She believes her husband and children exist in order to make her happy (though they have always failed). If her forty-year-old daughter eats something Mary considers fattening, Mary takes it as a personal slight. If her husband receives recognition from his professional peers, she feels slighted because he's getting attention she believes should be hers. Mary sees herself as the center of the universe. Those around her perpetually disappoint her. Angry, empty, and discontent, she'll never be happy—and it's all their fault.

Though her children earned the professional degrees she said she wanted, produced the grandchildren she said she wanted, visit her regularly, and accommodate her at every turn, they can never do enough. Though for fifty years her husband has loved, supported, and placated her, it's never been enough for Mary, who's always wanted more.

All her life she's felt empty and unhappy because she believes the world owes her the happiness she tries to take, but never tries to earn.

Though Michael lost his partner and then died young himself, he found the happiness that eludes Mary. He found fulfillment by sharing his special gifts with others, by making a positive difference in the world around him. When the church filled with a standing-room crowd, one could see though his life was cut short he did not live in vain. Michael gave of himself to the very end of his life, and by so doing filled himself up.

Take Personal Responsibility

In order to fill the void you feel inside, you must accept responsibility for filling it. If you expect others to do it for you, you'll stay empty. If you waste your energy resenting people for failing to make you happy, the void in you will deepen. But if you're willing to reach out, share what you have to give, and make a positive difference in the world around you, you will feel happier and gradually the void will disappear.

There Are Many Ways to Give of Yourself

How you give of yourself depends, in large part, on what you have to give. If your talents and interests are primarily artistic, you'll probably share yourself accordingly. If you are drawn to business, politics, or community service, that's probably where you can contribute most. If you're shy but eager to love and nurture, maybe you'll care for an animal, cultivate a close relationship with an elderly, housebound neighbor, or "adopt" a public school class in an underprivileged neighborhood.

Once you're ready to share what you have to give, simply devote the time, commit the energy, and start sharing.

Those of you drawn to active citizenship will find many opportunities to serve your community. When Burt's wife divorced him, he felt lonely and at loose ends. Retired but still active, Burt found reasons to go on living, sharing the skills and experience he'd accumulated over forty years. He volunteered at a center for the low-income elderly. He painted the recreation area, fixed the plumbing, and advised the center's director on how to improve the lighting. Sometimes he went to the apartments of people who came to the center and did odd jobs for them. By sharing his skills, Burt felt useful; by spending time with people who appreciated him, he stopped feeling lonely.

If you seek opportunities for companionship, hard work, and a sense of purpose, consider volunteering on a political campaign. When William left the Army, he moved to St. Louis, a city where he knew no one. A conscientious worker used to being busy, he felt useless and lonely. The man who lived in the apartment across the hall suggested he volunteer on a campaign. Though William was relatively apolitical, this idea aroused his curiosity. At first he just stuffed envelopes and rode around with other volunteers putting up yard signs. Later, he and another volunteer went doorbelling. The candidate appreciated William's work; William felt useful and made a lot of friends.

If you possess an aptitude for business, find an unfilled niche and fill it. When Alice's company merged with another, her job disappeared. Realizing she wouldn't find another like it, she inventoried her talents and interests and decided, after years of working for a big institution, she'd like to be her own boss. A good cook who enjoyed shopping for groceries, Alice determined that a business related to food made sense for her. Alice's family came from the Middle East, but she'd downplayed her ethnic origins in her old career. Now she decided to celebrate it and opened a store selling Middle Eastern foodstuffs and supplies. Her loyal clientele is growing and Alice enjoys being an entrepreneur. Alice found and filled an unfilled niche in the marketplace, shared what she had to give, and made a new and rewarding life for herself.

If you are a natural nurturer, you can do a lot of good caring for your friends and supporting your coworkers. Stephanie is the devoted mother of a son and daughter. Divorced by her husband when they were small, she was their primary parent for much of their early childhood and adolescence. Five years ago, tensions between her and her teenage daughter reached a breaking point, and the daughter moved in with her father. She cut off all contact with Stephanie and refused all Stephanie's efforts to restore a relationship. They are still estranged. This loss, needless to say, was crushing for her.

Stephanie responded by figuring out what was in her power to do. She *couldn't* control her daughter's feelings or responses. She *could* control her own actions. For five years, she has consistently and sensitively extended herself to her daughter. She has made it clear to her daughter that she will be welcome whenever she chooses to return.

Meanwhile, Stephanie has devoted herself to resolving old issues with her own parents and establishing a strong, loving relationship with them. She has developed an enviable friendship with her teenage son. Throughout this time she has been for me the most loyal and helpful friend and colleague imaginable. All this was within Stephanie's control to do. The results of her efforts have been to find love, loyalty, gratitude, professional influence, and the ability to look herself in the mirror with pride.

Joining one of the caring professions may be the best way to share your special talents. Eighteen-year-old Jessica couldn't stand living anymore, so she swallowed a bottle full of aspirin and passed out. Her brother found her and called for an ambulance. At the hospital, after she regained consciousness, the nurses went out of their way to make her feel special. The kindness of these women, their selfless tenderness toward a stranger, made a big impression on Jessica. She started focusing less on the shortcomings of her own life and started, for the first time, to think how she might help others. She decided to become a nurse. Her parents, delighted that she had broken out of her depression, happily paid Jessica's tuition. She did well in school, and in her spare time volunteered at the hospital, where she became increasingly aware of the joy caring for others can bring.

Pushing for legislation may be the way you can turn a negative into a positive. Alec's great-granddaughter died when a delivery truck backed over her. Desperate to find something positive in the death of this beloved little girl, Alec decided to do something to help protect other children from the same fate. Previously uninvolved in the political process, he started visiting the office of his state legislators, testified at hearings, and rounded up other interested and concerned citizens. His goal: legislation requiring trucks to make beeping sounds when they back up.

If you have the interest and the time and energy to give, caring for animals can bring you pleasure, companionship, and a sense of purpose. Barbara's work as a management consultant started taking an emotional toll. Drained by the crisis-filled work environments where she spent her days, she needed some relief. Though Barbara and her husband live in a city, their home is close to a ravine. This proximity to nature gave her the idea of creating a wildlife habitat in the backyard. Wildlife need food, water, and shelter. So to draw them to her yard, Barbara installed a birdbath among the trees and blackberry bushes. And she hung several bird feeders, each supplied with different feed, to draw particular species to her window. Caring for the independent, interesting, and sometimes beautiful creatures who now come to her yard calms, comforts, and rejuvenates her.

Kids of all ages need our support. If you want to help, you can in countless ways. In 1953, unmarried and absorbed in her work, my mother assumed she might never have children. Within a year she married and became stepmother to three children under seven. A year after that she had me, and seventeen months later, my brother Ben. Four years later, my sister Margaret was born. In 1960, she faced the challenge of five children under twelve, each with different interests and different needs, all pulling her in different directions. In the midst of attending to us, her identity began slipping away.

My mother started a day camp in our backyard. Children of all races and income levels attended. Teenagers served as counselors. Camp activities included art projects on the terrace and Greek plays in a corner of the yard, science experiments in the basement and gymnastics on the lawn. Day camp occupied and entertained us for that and many subsequent summers. In the process, my mother found relief from stress, some professional satisfaction, and a greater sense of self.

■

There is no one right way to share yourself. As long as you focus on what you can *contribute*, rather than on what you *want* from others, you'll do fine. Just figure out what you have to give, identify a need or an unfilled niche, and start contributing. Feeling useful, feeling you're making a positive difference in the world around you, is the best way I know to fill the void.

> *I don't know what your destiny will be,*
> *but one thing I know, the only ones among you*
> *who will be really happy*
> *are those who have sought and found how to serve.*
> ALBERT SCHWEITZER

Key Points:

- In order to fill the void you feel inside, you must accept responsibility for filling it. If you expect others to do it for you, it won't get filled.

- If you waste energy resenting others for not making you happy, the void you feel will deepen.

- If you're willing to reach out, share what you have to give, and make a positive difference in the world, you will feel happier, and, gradually, the void you feel inside will disappear.

- There are many ways to give of yourself. *How* you give depends in large part on *what* you have to give.

- You can make contributions through community or personal service, creativity, business, friendship, political volunteerism and legislative action, caring occupations, caring for animals, helping kids, and more.

7
Backsliding

Our greatest glory consists not in never falling,
but in rising every time we fall.
RALPH WALDO EMERSON

Raised to be a wife and mother, Pat defined her identity in relation to her family. After attending a southern college where she met her husband at a dance, she worked in an office to put him through graduate school and continued working until she got pregnant with twins. Then she focused on home: she took her children to the doctor, Scouts, and soccer practice, hosted dinner parties and organized summer picnics for her husband's firm. Trim, attractive, and busy, Pat felt happy with her life and secure about her future. Other couples divorced, but not Pat and Bob. They were different; they were solid. Their marriage would last forever.

By the time Pat was in her forties, the kids had finished college and were busy finding themselves. Bob spent more time at work and began to grow distant. One day he asked her to sit down and started to cry. He'd fallen in love with someone new and younger, a professional person like himself. When he moved in with the other woman, Pat remained alone in the house where they'd lived for twenty years. Bob left her comfortably provided for but lonely and lost. In a moment, her identity disappeared.

After her initial shock subsided, Pat picked herself up and began building a new life. Several women in the neighborhood went out of their way to support her, and she frequently joined them for dinners, day hikes, and evenings at the theater. She got a part-time secretarial job in a law firm and returned to college. On Fridays she either volunteered at a senior center or ran errands for a couple of housebound neighbors. Overall, she felt busy and useful.

Then, one day, as she walked down the street, Pat saw one of her three sons laughing with an attractive woman, a bit older than himself. She watched them for a while, standing by the entrance to a shop. Then Bob emerged and put his arm around the woman. She was *the one*. And Pat's son was laughing with her, laughing with this new young wife of Bob's. Pat felt betrayed, humiliated, alone, and devastated all over again.

For a while she felt all her work to build a new life had been for nothing. But she endured this fresh pain and once again picked herself up. She halted the downward spiral and nurtured herself with hot baths and weekly massage treatments. She resisted the temptation to gorge on sweets or drink too much, recommitted to a moderate, healthy diet, and got plenty of exercise. And she thought, Who can I help? Who needs an errand run? Who at the senior center would appreciate a visit? And as she reached out to others, family and friends again reached out to her. She began the journey to wholeness again, realizing this time the pain didn't last quite as long and the light in the distance shined a little closer than before.

∎

In general, the six steps should be taken consecutively. Day to day, however, the order of your steps may vary and you may backslide as often as you progress. In the course of a month you may feel pain one day, stabilize the next, look inward, feel better, then plummet once more, feel another wave of pain, resume your introspection, look outward, think you've finally recovered, then fall back again, and on and on. As you work through the process you may feel you are going in circles. Take heart! Backsliding is not only inevitable but, in an odd way, helpful.

Some steps are simply too difficult to accomplish completely at any one time. These you must experience in quantities you can bear. You cannot face up to your pain, or thoroughly look inward, all at once. You need relief, you need perspective. This you can obtain by halting the downward spiral, by looking outward, by sharing what you have to give. But then something will happen, and once again you will slide backward.

Filling the Void Is a Slow Process

Filling the void is a slow process of stops and starts, successes and disappointments, despair and hope. There are no shortcuts. People around you may try to rush you. They may think you should be over your husband's death, your infertility, your child's absence, your failed business. But if you still hurt, you still hurt. After my brother died, a colleague entered my office and asked how I was doing. "Not very well," I said. He responded, "When are you going to get over this thing? It's been two weeks. People are starting to talk." To him, the sensation of my brother's death had worn off. He felt ready to forget it and move on, so he expected me to do the same.

You may take years to fully recover or you may recover quickly. People differ, circumstances vary, and the time required to fill a void may be longer for one person than for another.

Times of Transition Can Be Valuable

Transitions take a while. Value exists not just in a destination but in the journey. Give yourself permission to take the time you need; don't feel ashamed for recovering more slowly than others think you should. If you diligently and deliberately work through the six steps, you will ultimately feel fulfilled and learn a lot along the way.

Triggers to a Backward Slide

Many things can trigger a backward slide. Holidays, weddings, and funerals, family visits and anniversaries often reopen wounds. So too, can the sight of a rival or adversary on the street. A news article, a book, a TV sitcom, or a film may revive old pain. A song on the radio evocative of a love long gone may leave you crying at a stop sign or as you drive along the interstate. Gray days, slow business, the flu, or lack of sleep may set you back as well. Whatever the trigger may be, you *will* slide backward.

A wedding brought together Alfredo's entire family. And for the first time in five years, he saw his father from whom he'd been estranged. Though happy to see his sisters, mother, aunts, and grandparents, the sight of his father made him anxious and upset. Feelings of shame, love, and regret evoked by the sight of his father left this otherwise contented individual exhausted and depressed.

Since their divorce, Roger and Pamela's kids spent Christmas Eve with Roger, and Christmas Day with Pamela and her new husband. Christmas morning used to be a special time for Roger: when the kids were little, he played Santa, made breakfast, and played Christmas carols on the piano. Now he usually spent Christmas mornings alone with the newspaper or working around the house. Though adjusted to the divorce and generally pretty happy, Roger suffered on Christmas mornings.

After the rape, Lily joined a support group and became politically active on behalf of sexual-assault victims. She resumed dating and overall felt happy and well-adjusted. But every year, near the anniversary of the rape, when the light looks as it did that late spring afternoon, and the air feels the same, and new green leaves cover the trees as they did that earlier, dreadful day, she remembers. And her anger and fear return to haunt her.

During their contentious divorce proceedings, Richard came to despise his wife's attorney. She bullied and antagonized him, challenged his integrity, and generally made his life miserable for several months. And to make things worse, his wife won custody of the kids and more than half their assets. Though Richard had recovered from his divorce, seeing this lawyer set him back, reviving his old hostility and resentment.

Jane felt lost and tearful for nearly a year after the last of her children left for college. But once she had settled comfortably into a new way of life, she felt surprised by her emotional reaction to a TV sitcom about a boy leaving for college; she cried inconsolably for nearly an hour.

The memory of dropping the ball and missing a touchdown during the last two minutes of the last game of his senior season haunted Jackson for a long time. Several years passed before he could watch a football game without wincing. But by his mid-twenties he had gained perspective, enjoyed watching games, and spent little time worrying about what might have been that December long ago. That was until he ran for a seat on the local school board and a reporter mentioned the ancient fumble in an article about Jackson's campaign. Then he felt humiliated and upset all over again.

When Nick left prison after serving time for cocaine possession, he committed himself to a sober, responsible life. He got a job, bought a home, married, and started a family. And he hardly remembered his two years of misery spent in the penitentiary until he read a novel that contained a vivid section on life behind bars. All the old feelings returned for a while, and several weeks passed before his depression lifted.

Hazel's neighbor lost her teenage son in an automobile accident. As a courtesy, Hazel attended his funeral. She did not expect to feel strong emotion for this boy she hardly knew. But sitting in the church, listening to the organ music, she was transported back to another funeral, her own son's, twenty years before. And she wept for him and all the years of living he had missed.

Backsliding Is Unpleasant and Discouraging, But Need Not Be Permanent

Backsliding can produce a variety of feelings, including anger and self-pity, sorrow and resentment. It may cause you to feel anxious about money or consumed with a desire for justice. Perhaps you will overeat or drink too much, turn up late for work, or accumulate traffic tickets. As you backslide, a tendency to blame others or look for rescuers may temporarily resurface. You may feel like a failure. If you do, you won't be alone. Many talented and successful people have met failure along the way. Winston Churchill twice failed the entrance exams to Sandhurst. Puccini's first music teacher said he had "no talent" and dropped him as a pupil. Albert Einstein's poor academic performance caused one of his teachers to suggest he drop out of school since he would never amount to anything. And before Abraham Lincoln became president of the United States, he lost a job, failed in private business, and lost campaigns for the legislature, land office, Congress, Senate and the vice presidency. So remember, though backsliding may produce ugly and unpleasant emotions, you need not feel defeated. Just find your balance and get back on track.

Methods for Getting Back on Track

Backsliding may revive your original feelings of emptiness, disappointment, or loss. When this happens, it helps to resume the six-step process. Halt the downward spiral in order to stabilize emotionally. Then, as you face up to pain in quantities you can endure, as you look inward and outward and go about sharing what you have to offer, certain techniques may help you stay on track.

Remember, filling the void you feel inside is *your* responsibility. If you dwell angrily on old, bitter memories or the recent conduct of someone who triggered your backward slide, you will not feel better. Try to focus on what is within your power to change. Waiting for others to rescue you, apologize, or make you happy is a waste of time. What can you do to make yourself feel better? What worked before? Walking in the mountains? Working in your garden? Listening to music? Getting a massage? If it worked for you before, start doing it again.

If you can see humor in your heartache, you are lucky. Art Buchwald observed, "I learned quickly that when I made others laugh, they liked me. This lesson I never forgot." If you can poke fun at your troubles and make yourself and others laugh at your predicament, you can bring a little light into your darkness. As James Thurber wrote, "Laughter need not be cut out of anything since it improves everything."

Without numbing yourself to the reality of your situation, it may help to create an impression of success and confidence even if you don't feel very confident or successful at the moment. The people around you usually will respond more positively if they feel you are strong and cheerful than if they perceive you as self-pitying and glum.

When actor Hugh Grant was caught with a prostitute in a car near Sunset Boulevard, the tabloids went wild. Grant no doubt felt tempted to slink into hiding—but he didn't. Instead he found the courage to take on the talk shows, apologize for his mistake, and even poke fun at himself. His wit, charm, and humility under pressure won him some sympathy and allowed him to carry on.

And when tennis great Arthur Ashe faced illness and personal attacks, he responded with dignity and grace. In order to compete in the all-white world of professional tennis, Ashe endured years of racist abuse. Consistently polite and dignified, he became the first African American ever to win the U.S. Open and Wimbledon championships, but his brilliant tennis career ended prematurely due to a bad heart. During surgery following one of three heart attacks, he contracted AIDS from a blood transfusion. Still, Ashe did not give up. He devoted the remainder of his life to helping others: young people, South Africans in search of freedom, Haitians hoping to flee their country, people living with AIDS, and his own friends and family.

Near the end, when he told the public he had AIDS, Arthur Ashe said, "Sure I think about death. But it doesn't frighten me. I never feel, 'Why me?' If I ask 'Why me?' about my troubles, I would have to ask 'Why me?' about my blessings. Why my winning Wimbledon? And why me marrying a beautiful, gifted woman and having a wonderful child?" (*People Weekly*, February 22, 1993). Throughout his ordeal he remained positive and principled. He was rewarded with the love of many friends and the admiration of millions.

The positive response you engender by creating an impression of confidence and good spirits may help you start *feeling* the way you *appear*. So, stand tall and smile the next time you walk down the street or into a meeting, and see what happens.

Remember—you've bounced back before! You will survive this, too. Your pain will ease and you'll start feeling better before long. At first, your good moments may seem fleeting, but in time they'll last longer, until one day you realize you actually feel good more often than you feel bad. In the earliest stages of grief, however, simply forgetting about your loss for the length of a movie or a ski slope is progress.

Stop acting like a victim; *search for your power*. If you feel powerless, think about what is *right* with your life. Write a list of your accomplishments, your strengths, and your resources, and start formulating a plan built on these. If you are unable to focus, ask a trusted friend or relative to help write it for you. Exercise what power you have to constructively advance your cause. Then reach out to those around you. Find ways to be useful. Share what you have to offer. As you do this, the tide will start to shift, and you will feel better and more hopeful.

After You Recover, There Will Remain a Spot That Can Still Hurt When It Is Pressed

When Steve's wife left him for his best friend, a wise and sympathetic person told him, "In time you will be happy again. In time you will heal. But there will always be a spot on you that hurts when it is pressed. The spot will shrink but it will never completely go away."

When you recover from a great loss or disappointment, though you feel full of purpose and happy, you still may backslide once in a while. Twelve years after my brother's death, my husband and I went to the film *A River Runs Through It*. Its story of a vital, beautiful, wayward brother who died violently and young affected me deeply. More than anything I'd read or seen in the intervening years, it brought back vivid memories of my brother's life and death, and when we returned to the car, I wept. But this experience did not pull me down; it helped release my lingering grief.

Backsliding Is Therapeutic

Backsliding is part of the recovery process, and as unpleasant as it may be, it can be therapeutic. Since you must face up to all your pain in order to fully recover, but can only endure it in bearable quantities, backsliding ensures you'll continue to confront all the pain requiring your attention.

Feeling discouraged for repeatedly slipping back is understandable. But anyone overcoming a great loss slips back. And each time you start again your journey will be a little shorter, your destination a little closer. Try not to let other people's schedules for your recovery upset you. As bad as you feel when you slide backward, the feelings will not last. The time you spend feeling bad will shrink and your progress will hasten.

There will always be experiences that can trigger a backward slide. But each time you slide backward, you'll learn something new. And each time, you'll find a way back on course.

Key Points:

- Backsliding is inevitable and therapeutic.

- Some steps are simply too difficult to accomplish completely at any one time. These you must accomplish in quantities you can bear.

- Filling the void is a slow process of stops and starts, successes and disappointments, despair and hope. There are no shortcuts.

- Don't let yourself be rushed (but don't languish in self-pity).

- What sets you back will sometimes be obvious, other times surprising. Triggers that may lead to a backward slide include: holidays, weddings, funerals, anniversaries, the sight of an adversary, news articles, TV, books, films, songs on the radio, and more.

- Backsliding is unpleasant and discouraging but not permanent.

- Methods for getting back on track include:

  - *Resuming the six-step process*

  - *Humor*

  - *Creating an impression of confidence and success*

- *Visualization*

- *Writing lists of what is right with your life, your accomplishments, your strengths, and your resources*

- *Focusing on what is within your power to affect*

- After you recover, there will remain a spot that still hurts when it is pressed. The spot will shrink but it will never completely go away.

- After a great loss or disappointment, there will always be experiences that can trigger a backward slide. Each time you will learn something, each time you will find a way back on course, and the light in the distance will shine a little closer than before.

8

Finding Fulfillment

*Happiness is mostly a by-product of doing
what makes us feel fulfilled.*
BENJAMIN SPOCK

In just three years, my grandmother (whom we called Mamie)
lost the three principal men in her life: her father when she
was thirty-seven, her brother at thirty-nine, and her husband
at forty. When her husband died in 1932, she faced the responsibility of completing the upbringing of their three young children with no one to help her. She had not gone to college, could
not type or cook, and had never held a paying job. With neither
experience nor formal training, she took over the family's property management business. This involved managing a largely
empty office building and several smaller properties, at a time
when business was poor and tenants, struggling through the
Depression, were desperate.

Mamie was handicapped not only by ignorance but by the difficulty of dealing with other business executives, all of whom

were men. Some refused to deal with her because they felt inhib-
ited from shouting and pounding on the table, and others she
would not deal with because they insisted on shouting and
pounding on the table. On the other hand, some went out of their
way to help her, in part because as she was a woman, they did
not regard her as a competitor.

Mamie ultimately succeeded in the real estate business. Then,
in the 1940s, she cashed in most of her property and gambled on
a new and largely untested business venture: television. She
bought a money-losing radio station and a fledgling television
station, and built them into a large, complex broadcasting business, eventually serving millions of consumers in several states.

When Mamie looked inward, she discovered a great talent for
business. For over forty years she expressed it through business
and community leadership. Tragedy led her to discover her
genius, and hard work and luck allowed her to realize it fully.

My grandmother found great fulfillment in her business. But
the pain of losing the men she loved coupled with pressure to
earn a living proved, for a long time, too much for her consciously to bear. For years she shut down emotionally and
poured herself into work. But pain cannot be avoided forever. So
late in life she faced her ancient pain and the consequences of
ignoring it for so long.

When Mamie was in her early eighties, all three of her middle-
aged children left their marriages in the course of a single year. I
remember the surprise I felt as a twenty-one-year-old when my
strong, steady grandmother cried in my arms. She said she felt
responsible for her children's broken marriages. Having buried
herself in business following the death of her husband, Mamie realized she had failed her children in some very important ways.
Though she had provided each of them with financial security and
a fine education, she had neglected their emotional needs.

"I was neither suited to childrearing nor interested in house-
work," she admitted. But when fate thrust her into the unfamiliar
world of business she realized it had presented her with the

opportunity to finally fulfill her potential. Having never been a very good mother, she elected to devote the next forty years of her life to what she did best.

Although facing up to her deficiencies as a parent obviously caused Mamie pain, confronting what was really troubling her seemed to give her the impetus to transform herself into a more broadly focused, more loving person. During the last decade of her life, she became warmer, more sensitive, flexible, and complete. That is the woman I remember and whose name I'm proud to share.

How and When You Find Fulfillment Will Vary, Depending Upon Your Circumstances

Finding fulfillment is a process, not a prize won at the end of a competition. Some people find fulfillment more easily than others. One person may sustain an enormous loss, such as the suicide of a spouse, but find happiness within a relatively short period of time. Another person may sustain a loss objectively much smaller, such as failure to achieve a desired level of professional success, but take longer to find fulfillment. We don't all start from the same place. Someone with a happy childhood, loving friends, and financial security who sustains a great loss or disappointment may find fulfillment more easily than someone without these advantages. And if an individual sustains multiple losses in quick succession (e.g., the death of a parent, the loss of a job, and a divorce), fulfillment is likely to be much harder to find than it would be for someone who experiences a single loss. If you believe your troubles are due in part to a chemical imbalance (e.g., manic depression or an anxiety disorder), discuss with your physician whether there is medication that might help you. Then, despite these variables, if you exercise self-discipline and patiently work through each of the six steps, I believe that though your journey may be long and difficult, you ultimately will find the fulfillment you seek.

To Find Fulfillment You Must First Create It

Man's main task in life is to give birth to himself.

ERICH FROMM

To find fulfillment you must first determine what is important to you. If you can't think what that is, why not try writing your own brief biography? How do you think you would be remembered were you to die today? Is that how you want to be remembered? If not, write your ideal biography. What do you want to be remembered for? "She created beauty." "He was kind to children." "She served God." "He served his community." "She made people laugh." After writing this, imagine lying on your deathbed, and look back over your life. What mattered? What didn't? What made you proud? What do you regret? What do you wish you'd done differently? Do you wish you had spent more time with your parents, worked harder, played more, spent better quality time with your kids, loved more, made more time for friends? (When a group of individuals in their nineties was surveyed about what they wished they'd done differently, a majority responded that if they could live their lives over, they would risk more, reflect more, and create something of enduring value.) By writing your ideal biography and by reflecting about your life as you might on your deathbed, you will define a vision for living.

Once you develop a vision for your life, ask yourself what values or beliefs guide you. Will they help you live the life you want to live? If you want to be remembered for kindness to your fellow man but the value actually governing your daily life is "to make as much money as possible," you may need to rethink and reprioritize your values. To "love thy neighbor as thyself" may be the value better able to help you live the life you say you want.

Keep alert to deeply held beliefs that prevent you from living the life you want. If you believe "I must be perfect," "I don't deserve to be happy," "I need to be right," or "Other people are supposed to take care of me," you will find it difficult to live the life you want to be remembered for. Your challenge will be to change your belief system so that it reinforces rather than undermines your vision.

Changing your belief system will be difficult. Sources of support include religious and philosophic texts, spiritual counselors, psychotherapists, and certain self-help books. Those people I know who have successfully changed their systems of belief proceeded in various ways. Some adopted a religion or political philosophy; others modeled themselves after individuals they admired; and still others employed the techniques of cognitive and behavioral therapy.

Doug significantly reduced his passive-aggressive behavior, his tendency to procrastinate, and his "need to be right" by consulting with a psychologist who specialized in rational-emotive therapy (RET) and by reading books such as *When I Say No I Feel Guilty*, by Manuel J. Smith (Bantam Books, 1985), *A New Guide to Rational Living*, by Albert Ellis, Ph.D. and Robert Harper, Ph.D. (Wilshire Book Company, 1975), and *Overcoming Procrastination*, by Albert Ellis, Ph.D., and William Frause, Ph.D. (a Signet Book, The Penguin Group, 1977). RET provided him with a framework for examining then minimizing those beliefs which were preventing him from achieving his goals. It also gave him tools and a rationale for developing the skills he needed to become more effective in his personal and professional relationships. With time and effort, he changed the way he thought, reacted, and behaved, and became a happier, more successful (and more likable) man.

Once you decide on a vision and clarify your values, set some goals for yourself. If you want to be remembered for serving your community, you could start by setting a goal to volunteer once a month at a hospital, community center, or school. Then do it. If you wish you spent better quality time with your children, you could start by setting a goal to spend more time with them. Then make the time. Whatever your vision, whatever your values, setting and meeting goals that reinforce and advance your vision

and remain true to your values will help you create the fulfillment you seek.

Convert Emptiness into Energy, Pain into Power, Self-Doubt into Self-Worth, and Suffering into Service

Emptiness, pain, suffering, and self-doubt afflict rich and poor,
old and young, every race, every creed . . . everyone. In the midst
of your troubles you may feel alone. You may feel that no one
ever suffered as much as you have. But you need only look
closely at your neighbors to realize they have suffered, too.

Sharon's fiancé decided to move to a new city. Since she wanted
to be with him, Sharon and her fourteen-year-old daughter left everyone and everything they knew and moved a thousand miles away.
There she exchanged her successful corporate identity for a blank
slate. Long interested in environmental protection, she threw herself into the environmental movement, gaining expertise and earning respect in the area of nuclear waste clean-up. Sharon led large
tree-planting projects, organized educational programs, and
coproduced a book to help businesses become environmentally
responsible. A natural leader, she motivated hundreds of people to
join her in these and other projects. In the process, she converted
her emptiness into energy and found personal fulfillment. The
place that once felt foreign became "home."

Born with cerebral palsy, Bud always spoke haltingly and
shook uncontrollably. But his parents believed in his potential
and so did he. Raised in Boston, he loved watching hockey and
wanted to play. At age eleven he approached the school's hockey
coach and asked to join the team. "But you can't play hockey,"
he said. "You shake." Bud felt crushed, but his brother quickly
devised a solution: Bud could play goalie and put his uncontrollable shaking to good use. He joined the hockey team and played
for many years. Throughout his life, Bud has converted his pain

into power. Now he makes a living as a popular motivational speaker, telling audiences inspirational tales of his life and inspiring them to make more of their own.

Much in Maria's life caused her self-doubt. Raised in a barrio, where she spoke only street Spanish, she found schoolwork, particularly English, difficult. Long ago abandoned by her father, her irresponsible, heroin-addicted mother was all she had for a parent. Various men passed through her mother's life, occasionally abusing Maria along the way. And more children came, half-siblings, whom Maria felt obliged to raise.

In spite of these obstacles, Maria found ways to convert her self-doubt into self-worth and pull herself up from her oppressive circumstances. At school she sought out mentors, responsible adults, teachers, and staff from whom she learned a different, better set of values. She made an effort to assist these people, by helping them out around the classroom and in the office. Always courteous, conscientious, and obliging, she became invaluable to her admiring mentors. They believed in her and, in time, she began believing in herself.

When Jim lost a much-loved brother in World War II he was virtually immobilized by grief. His wife urged him to convert his suffering into service and honor his brother's memory by dedicating himself to improving the community where they grew up. For half a century he's done just that. He spearheaded the cleanup of Lake Washington and led successful efforts to build a downtown Convention Center and an urban park across the freeway. Because of him the county launched a major system of parks and trails; because of him there are hundreds of units of new low-income housing; and because of him thousands of acres of open space will be preserved in a greenway across the Cascade Mountains. Tragedy caused Jim to do great things for his community and in the process bring great honor to his cherished brother's memory.

As you can see, there are many ways to find fulfillment. Your circumstances will determine the length, difficulty, and course of your journey, but if you persevere and diligently complete each of the six steps, you can find it.

> *Many persons have a wrong idea of what constitutes*
> *true happiness. It is not attained through self-grat-*
> *ification but through fidelity to a worthy purpose.*
> HELEN KELLER

Blind, deaf, and unable to speak, Helen Keller still managed to pursue a worthwhile purpose, make a contribution, and find fulfillment. Sharon, Jim, Maria, Bud, and Mamie each overcame adversity, shared themselves, and found fulfillment. And so can you. By identifying what you have to offer and conscientiously pursuing a worthwhile purpose outside yourself, you too can successfully overcome challenging circumstances, fill the void you feel inside, and find fulfillment.

Key Points:

- Finding fulfillment is a process, not a prize won at the end of a competition.

- To find fulfillment you must first create it.

- By determining what is important to you, you define a vision for living.

- Set goals that advance your vision and remain true to your values.

- Some people find fulfillment faster and more easily than others.

- In the midst of your troubles, you may feel no one ever suffered as much as you have. But all you need to do is look closely at your neighbors to realize they have suffered too.

- Your circumstances will determine the length, difficulty, and course of your journey, but if you persevere and diligently complete each of the six steps, you can fill the void and find fulfillment.

9
A Way of Life

He that would have the fruit must climb the tree.

DR. THOMAS FULLER

D illy Mae found a way of living that keeps her happy and fulfilled.

Born around the turn of the century to a family of Texas sharecroppers, she grew up working in corn and cotton fields. As a young woman, the man she loved broke her heart. Strong, self-confident, and trusting in God, she picked herself up and moved on. She stopped working as a sharecropper, became a domestic worker for four dollars a week, and started saving for the future.

After World War II, she met Edgar, a nondrinking, hardworking man who proved a loyal husband for half a century. "I don't have a lazy bone in my body," says Edgar, now in his nineties. He began by stacking wood for fifty cents a cord and picking cotton for a dollar a day. As a young man he shined shoes, washed dishes, baked pies, and, when war broke out, joined the Army. After serving in World War II, Edgar returned home, matured and ready for commitment.

He and Dilly Mae married and moved north. Between them
they had a suitcase, a box, and fifty dollars. Though neither
could read, they made a good life for themselves. She cooked,
cleaned, and sewed for a living; she collected scraps of cloth for
homemade quilts and crocheted pillows and blankets. For thirteen years Edgar never missed a day working on the floor of a
street-broom factory. Later, he bought a truck and delivered
goods, did odd jobs, and helped people move.

Dilly Mae took care of the money. She squirreled away enough
for them to buy a house. Edgar survived on a cup of coffee and a
hamburger until dinner in order to keep down expenses. In time
they bought a second house and then a third, earning additional
income by renting out rooms.

Church has always been at the center of Dilly Mae's life. For
years she sang in the gospel choir. And she's always helped people in need in her church and neighborhood. Both Edgar and
Dilly Mae live by the Golden Rule: "Do unto others as you would
have them do unto you." They believe this attitude is what
brought them happy lives.

Though they wanted to have children, they couldn't. Instead they
gave love and attention to countless children in their community,
becoming surrogate parents and grandparents to many. On a
recent Mother's Day, their church honored Dilly Mae. One parish-
ioner commented, "But she has no children." To which the person
beside him responded, "She has lots of children, and I am one."

Dilly Mae has led a happy life because she learned early how
to play to her strengths and find joy within herself and in service
to others. Though she has had heart attacks and extensive
surgery, and Edgar is nearly blind, Dilly Mae remains self-suffi-
cient and content. She takes care of her husband, goes to church,
enjoys the friendship and support of the many people whose
admiration and gratitude she's earned, and does the work she
loves: cooking, quilting, and sewing children's clothes. Sewing,
she says, releases her mind from life's pressures.

Her life is one of diligence, dignity, generosity, and faith.

Wasting little time worrying about her misfortunes, Dilly Mae takes time to enjoy and appreciate what life has given her.

■

Once you have successfully recovered from a broken heart, shattered identity, or deep sense of emptiness, you won't enjoy the luxury of simply marching through the remainder of your life. Frustrating as it may be, life is not static. New things keep happening. New disappointments, frustrations, and losses will befall you no matter how well you've recovered from what came before. In order to build on what you've accomplished and maximize your overall happiness, you need to translate the steps you've taken into a way of life.

Developing the Following Habits Will Help You Cope with Future Challenges:

- Routinely nurture your body, soothe your soul, and, if, possible, continue relieving yourself of unnecessary pressures.

- Deal directly with problems as they arise.

- Seek guidance and support from a higher power.

- Strive to forgive those whom you waste time and energy resenting.

- Practice compassion.

- Forgive yourself for your imperfections.

- Resist slipping into self-absorption.

- Keep alert to interests you might develop.

- Keep a lookout for opportunities to express your talents; take them.

- Continue sharing what you have to offer with others.

- "Do unto others as you would have them do unto you."

Pay attention to the techniques that have helped you effectively halt the downward spiral. Make them a part of your routine. If regular exercise, time outdoors, someone to cut your lawn, and a moderate diet helped stabilize you when you were in crisis, they can cushion you the next time you fall. Think of the techniques you used to nurture your body, soothe your soul, and relieve yourself of unnecessary pressures, in order to store up energy and peace of mind that will enable you to handle the future blows life inevitably will inflict.

Dealing directly with problems as they arise will help prevent minor difficulties from escalating into overwhelming ones and prepare you to face up to tragedy if it comes.

Strive to resolve the significant relationships in your life. Ask yourself: if your parent, child, or spouse died tomorrow, would you be at peace in remembering your relationship? If not, what can you do *right now* to make it better? What can you do to achieve some degree of resolution? Do what you can before it is too late.

Even if you doubt the existence of God, asking for guidance and support as you drop off to sleep at night may bring you comfort and a sense of direction. And when your life is jolted by new and unexpected crises, this practice should make you feel less lonely and frightened as you face each challenge.

If you, like me, place great importance on justice and fair dealing, it may be difficult not to feel angry or resentful toward those who wronged you or your loved ones. But if you become obsessed by bitter resentment, a desire for revenge, or a need to right wrongs outside your power to correct, you may become immobilized. Learning how to forgive but not forget, accept but not condone, let go and do the good within your power to accomplish will free you to move forward.

Try to be compassionate—toward yourself as well as others. The Dalai Lama says, "If you want others to be happy, practice compassion. If you want to be happy, practice compassion."

Mark Twain observed, "A man cannot be comfortable without his own approval." If you tend to be your own harshest critic, let up a little. Are you taking responsibility for things outside your power to accomplish? If so, find ways to increase your power or reduce your level of responsibility. When authority and responsibility don't match, it's natural to feel stressed and down on yourself. Strive to be someone you're proud to see in the bathroom mirror and be kind to yourself. Forgive yourself for your imperfections. If you do, when big losses and disappointments occur and you're sapped of the energy required to perform up to your usual standards, you won't feel as badly.

People seem to me most miserable when they're obsessed by what's wrong in their lives. When I feel this way, I try to move outside myself. I ask, "How can I be useful? Who can I help?" By reaching out, by being useful, by helping someone else— writing a letter of sympathy or working on a community project, helping out a friend or doing something special for someone I care about—I feel better. By reaching out to others you will cultivate relationships; you will build a support system. And next time you fall, chances are people will be there to help you up.

If you know someone in trouble, too proud to ask for help, take a risk and offer your hand; perhaps he'll take it. And if you, too, tend to hide away in painful solitude when times get tough, consider asking your friends to seek you out the next time you "disappear."

Michelle survived domestic abuse, divorce, bankruptcy, and the loss of her job. She overcame alcoholism, launched a new career, and rebuilt a good life for herself and her child. Now, each night before she goes to bed, she sits down with a pen and paper and answers the following questions:

> *What have I done for others today?*
>
> *What have I done to take care of myself?*
>
> *What, if anything, am I upset about? And, what can I do about it?*
>
> *Why am I glad to be alive?*

Even when you've recovered from your current loss, remain alert to interests you might develop and unexploited talents you might express. Valuable opportunities may present themselves. If they do, seize them. Feeling useful or creative can bring great joy and do much to maintain a life worth living during difficult times.

Continue sharing what you have to offer. Reaching outside yourself will help free you from the burden of excessive preoccupation with life's limitations and remind you instead of life's bounty.

Building the six steps into your daily life will help prepare you for the next crisis, disappointment, or loss. This can provide you with a foundation of stability from which to respond faster and more effectively to problems as they arise. A body as healthy as possible, a serene soul, a clear sense of identity, and the ability to move outside yourself and share your special gifts will make life unfold more easily and maximize your happiness.

Key Points:

- Once you successfully recover from a broken heart, shattered identity, or a deep sense of emptiness, you won't enjoy the luxury of simply marching through the remainder of your life.

- Life is not static; new things keep happening. New disappointments, frustrations, and losses will befall you no matter how well you've recovered from what came before.

- Developing certain habits can help you cope with future challenges:

  - *Routinely nurture your body, soothe your soul, and, if, possible, continue relieving yourself of unnecessary pressures.*

  - *Deal directly with problems as they arise.*

  - *Seek guidance and support from a higher power.*

  - *Strive to forgive those whom you waste time and energy resenting.*

  - *Practice compassion.*

  - *Forgive yourself for your imperfections.*

  - *Try to be someone you're proud to see in the bathroom mirror.*

  - *Resist slipping into self-absorption.*

  - *Keep alert to interests you might develop.*

  - *Keep an eye out for opportunities to express your talents—and take them.*

  - *Continue sharing what you have to offer with others.*

  - *"Do unto others as you would have them do unto you."*

10
Building
a Better World as
We Heal Ourselves

*Why build these cities glorious
If man unbuilded goes?
In vain we build the world, unless
The builder also grows.*

EDWIN MARKHAM

After beginning my career as a trial lawyer, I was persuaded to leave law practice to manage my family's ski areas and property management business. I earned my M.B.A. and redefined myself as a businessperson, gradually shedding my previous identity. After seven years, I reached the point where managing a large organization, mentoring employees, and protecting and growing my family's assets *were* my identity. Since my husband and I have no children, I focused nearly all my maternal feelings on my employees, individuals for whom

I felt respect and great affection. I expected to stay with them, in that company, for the rest of my life. But I didn't.

A conflict with my father (my boss and the largest stockholder) over the company's direction resulted in my leaving, suddenly and unexpectedly. When I left, I left behind my identity and a large piece of my heart.

I turned once again to my mother's example for guidance and support. With difficulty, I gradually accepted that I would never return to my old life. With the unwavering support of my husband, mother, and younger sister, friends and many former employees, I set out to build a new life of which I could be proud.

Stephanie, my friend and personal assistant, always wants to know how books end before she reads them. But she took a risk and joined me on an uncertain journey with no known destination. Her faith in me and willingness to help me build a new business and a new life helped keep me stable and on track. Since we lacked capital to buy an existing business, we started one from scratch, a management consulting business designed to allow me to blend skills I had developed as a lawyer with those I had acquired as a business executive.

Like most start-up ventures, we predicted (correctly) the business would take a while to build. So to keep myself busy, usefully employ my skills, and rebuild my shattered identity, I did what my mother always did—I found ways to serve my community. She had taught me the best way to recover from personal loss is to do what one can to help build a better world. And she was right.

Finding Ways to Serve

Always active in the community, I significantly increased my involvement. I worked on a number of political campaigns and chaired several community projects; one of these was United Neighbors Investing Through Youth. The UNITY Project took more of my time, energy, and skills than any other pursuit. It also brought me the greatest rewards.

In 1992, following the first Rodney King trial verdict, when Los Angeles burst into flames and local youth tore through downtown Seattle, breaking windows and setting fires, I wanted to do something. As a businessperson and as a citizen, I wanted to help reconcile my divided city.

It was my perception that unilateral charity or "handouts" given to the poor and disenfranchised had failed to build self-worth, break the poverty cycle, or heal communities. The UNITY Project, which I conceived and chaired, was designed to move away from that imperfect benefactor-beneficiary model for addressing social problems and toward a partnership approach through which people of different races, cultures, and income levels together could accomplish something tangible and worthwhile, unachieveable by any one partner acting alone.

The UNITY Project brought together a thousand volunteers from all walks of life. Residents of a local housing project, working side by side with business people, artists, and social service providers, renovated and expanded a YMCA and created a state-of-the-art children's playground in the heart of one of the city's poorest, most racially divided and violent neighborhoods.

It began with a conversation with five teenagers. I asked, "What would you like to see done to physically improve your neighborhood? Would you be willing to help make it happen?" In response, the teenagers started meeting weekly with a team of volunteer architects, engineers, and contractors. The kids (whose numbers grew each week) determined what they wanted. They made all the policy choices for the YMCA and children's playground, and then the volunteer design team translated their vision into a workable plan.

The process was not always smooth. At one meeting a young man angrily responded to my suggestion that residents join with businesspeople to paint, hammer nails, move lumber, and clean up the neighborhood. I told him the project was built around the premise that all participants would donate something of value. Architects would donate designs; businesses, construction materials and equipment; residents, time and ideas. Everyone would donate labor. He said it was outrageous to expect residents to volunteer. They should be paid. He insisted that the business-people should donate time, materials, money, and expertise, but that the residents were entitled to receive these benefits without contributing anything in return.

The other teens challenged him. They said no one owed them charity. They were embarrassed by the young man's outburst, his claim of entitlement. This conflict motivated the committed teenagers to recruit others in order to fulfill their end of the bargain. Hundreds of residents, including seventy-five teenagers, ultimately volunteered.

In spite of their commitment, many of the teenagers—hardened by previous disappointments and broken promises—doubted the business-community partners would fulfill their end of the bargain. With this in mind, businesspeople who volunteered were told it was imperative they follow through on any promises made to these kids. Whether their promises were large or small, follow-through was critical to establishing trust, demonstrating respect, and giving the participating residents a sense of power. In time, the teens' skepticism was replaced by optimism and enthusiasm.

Because of UNITY there are now cooking classes in the brand-new center that includes a kitchen, movies, and much more. Kids are exercising in the renovated gym, the new weight room, and out on the playground. Money continues flowing into the neighborhood from individuals, businesses, government agencies, and foundations. There has been no vandalism; the community has protected and preserved what the project created—because residents feel a new sense of ownership and responsibility. And some kids who used to be ashamed of their neighborhood now say they feel proud to live there.

Searching for Purpose

Of all the volunteers, the most committed were Makda and Charlie. Makda was thirteen when her family emigrated from the Sudan and moved into the housing project. Her parents spoke no English and could not find work. The new kid in the neighborhood and the new kid at school, she started searching for a new purpose in life.

When Charlie retired, he expected to travel all over the world with his wife of nearly fifty years. But they didn't. Marie suffered a stroke which left her nearly blind and severely depressed, so they stayed home. Full of energy and ambition with nowhere to put it, Charlie, like Makda, looked for a new purpose in life. They found it together.

Through the Rotary Club, Charlie, a seventy-six-year-old retired general contractor, got involved with the UNITY Project. As the volunteer project coordinator, he worked six days a week for nearly two years. He made sure the project had all the necessary permits, that construction proceeded logically, safely, and under skilled supervision, and that the materials and equipment used were of the highest quality. Quality, he said, was a sign of respect.

In addition to helping recruit hundreds of businesspeople and tradesmen to volunteer time, materials, and expertise, Charlie mentored the neighborhood teenagers who wanted to help. One such volunteer was fourteen-year-old Makda, who in addition to maintaining her studies and family responsibilities wanted to make her neighborhood a safer, more attractive place to live. Makda volunteered for over a year on UNITY. She designed and built a staircase, installed insulation, and framed, plastered, and painted walls. Later, she established a teen-run club called The Future Is Ours, which offers children ages five to twelve role models, education, entertainment, and an alternative to the life of gangs and violence chosen by many neighborhood youth.

Reaping Rewards

Makda and Charlie became a team. Day after day they worked together on UNITY, and, later, the childrens' club. In the process they became friends. Unsolicited, Charlie sent Makda's high school counselor a letter of recommendation to help her get jobs and into college. He took her to concerts, nominated her for awards, and helped her and her father get work. She became a loyal and enthusiastic friend to Charlie and his wife, whom Makda helped care for during her last months of life. Makda says, "I've learned a lot of things from Charlie: wisdom, knowledge, self-confidence, and more. Every time I see Charlie I just hope that the world has more like him."

Charlie and Makda crossed generations, race, income, and culture to become friends, because they share the common values of industry, responsibility, integrity, and service. They both moved outside themselves to help build a better world. In the process they found fulfillment. And so did I. My work on the UNITY Project allowed me to use and improve my management, advocacy, and writing skills, to expand my network of relationships, to contribute to my community, and to feel a great sense of purpose and accomplishment.

Overcoming Obstacles to a Brighter Future

As a result of UNITY and other work I've done to help bring people together, the mayor of Seattle asked me to speak about peace at a United Nations Day event. Preparing for my speech, I thought a lot about what makes neighbors fight and nations go to war. In the process, I realized the causes of war and urban violence in many ways resemble the obstacles that confront individuals recovering from personal loss and disappointment, obstacles I too had to overcome.

W. E. B. DuBois, in his prophetic 1903 classic, *The Souls of Black Folk** (rpt; Bantam Books, 1989) which anticipated much of the African American consciousness and activism of the 1960s, wrote,

> The question of the future is how best to keep . . .
> millions from brooding over the wrongs of the

> past and the difficulties of the present, so that all
> their energies may be bent toward a cheerful
> striving and cooperation with their . . . neighbors
> toward a larger, juster and fuller future.

His words apply to those of us who cannot move forward because of our fixation on past injuries and the present difficulties they have helped to produce. The process an individual must go through to rebuild a shattered identity or heal a broken heart is not unlike that required to rebuild a city divided by urban strife or a nation exhausted by war. Each is a slow and challenging process. Each requires forgiveness, patience, generosity, and hard work. Only then can an individual or a community really focus on a bright and better future.

That was my challenge, and with opportunities for service, guidance from a higher power, and the love of friends and relatives, eventually I found my bright and better future. After my long and difficult journey, I looked back over the road I'd taken and identified the steps that had led me through the darkness into light: I halted my downward spiral, faced my pain, looked inward and then outward, shared what I had to give, slid backward again and again, and, ultimately, found fulfillment, even joy.

Converting Loss into a Force for Good

Examples of people who converted loss and disappointment into a force for good fill the pages of this book. Through community service and artistic expression, job creation and provision of quality goods and services, acts of generosity and lasting friendship, they built a better world. And as they moved outside themselves and shared their particular gifts, they found fulfillment.

Loss spurred my mother, Jim, and Sharon to serve their communities. By working for a united city and a peaceful world, my mother has touched thousands of lives and added immeasurable value to the world around her. Jim has honored his brother's memory with a half-century of priceless civic leadership. And Sharon is helping to save the earth.

Fred transformed his grief over his daughter's death, Michael, his anxiety about a grave illness, and Christine, her general discontent into artistic inspiration, expressed through dance, film, and painting. And as they filled the void inside themselves, they entertained, educated, and enriched their audiences.

When fate forced them to start over, Merle, Mamie, and Alice discovered hidden talents for business. Because they responded to their losses by sharing their special gifts, thousands of people were employed and countless customers served.

Others found ways to help those who suffered as they had. Andrea counseled men and women who, like her, were challenged by eating disorders. Kate helped battered wives after experiencing her own domestic abuse. And Michael, whose partner died of AIDS and who would himself eventually die of the disease, counseled and comforted people with AIDS and their survivors.

Making the world better requires no grand gesture or dramatic accomplishment. A loyal and compassionate friend like Stephanie, a helpful student like Maria, or a generous neighbor like Dilly Mae make real contributions. Everyone has a gift. If you have a void inside, sharing what you have to offer will help fill it. In the process *you will improve the world.*

> *To laugh often and love much, to win the respect of intelligent persons and the affection of children; to earn the approbation of honest critics and to endure the betrayal of false friends; to appreciate beauty; to find the best in others; to give one's self; to leave the world a bit better, whether by a healthy child, a garden patch or a redeemed social condition; to have played and laughed with enthusiasm and sung with exultation; to know even one life has breathed easier because you have lived, this is to have succeeded.*
>
> RALPH WALDO EMERSON

Filling the Void

You can move from a state of emptiness and despair to a state of fulfillment and joy, if you commit to a positive path and resist the temptation to dwell on disappointment, seek revenge, or succumb to self-pity.

As one door shuts in your face, resist the temptation to pound on that door—it may be closed forever. Look around for an open window or another, more accessible door.

What is within your control? What good is within your power to create? At the moment you feel most impotent, do not ignore the power that is yours to exercise—the power that will come if you allow yourself to focus on what you *can* do, rather than dwell on what has been done to you or what you *cannot* do.

This course can bring countless rewards and help you heal.

Key Points

- Focus on what you *can* do rather then dwell on what has been done *to* you or what you *cannot* do.

- Fill the void inside your heart by sharing your particular gifts with others.

- Remember the six steps:

  1. *Halt the downward spiral.*

  2. *Face your pain.*

  3. *Look inward.*

  4. *Look outward.*

  5. *Share what you have to give.*

  6. *Find fulfillment.*

About the Author

Dorothy Bullitt knows about loss firsthand: her brother was drowned, her niece committed suicide, and her professional identity was nearly destroyed when personal and business conflicts forced her to leave her family's company. She wrote this book when she couldn't find another that truly spoke to her when she was in crisis. She wanted to help the reader heal just as she did. As a management consultant, Bullitt draws on her experience as a lawyer and business executive to help organizations find new ways to achieve success, and to counsel individuals about career advancement, and work and life transitions. Bullitt and her husband live in Seattle.